W9-BVB-666

Cooking *for* Madam

Recipes and Reminiscences from the Home of Jacqueline Kennedy Onassis

MARTA SGUBIN

and Nancy Nicholas

A LISA DREW BOOK

SCRIBNER

A LISA DREW BOOK / SCRIBNER
1230 Avenue of the Americas
New York, NY 10020

Set in Simoncini Garamond

BOOK DESIGN BY RENATO STANISIC

Manufactured in the United States of America

1 3 5 7 9 10 8 6 4 2

Library of Congress Cataloging-in-Publication Data
Sgubin, Marta.
Cooking for madam : recipes and reminiscences from the home of
Jacqueline Kennedy Onassis / Marta Sgubin and Nancy Nicholas.
p. cm.
"A Lisa Drew book."
Includes index.
1. Cookery. 2. Onassis, Jacqueline Kennedy, date.
I. Nicholas, Nancy. II. Title.
TX714.S49 1998
641.5—dc21 98-24678
CIP

ISBN 0-684-85005-2

Photo Credits

Cover: Linen tray set by D. Porthault; tortoiseshell tray from William Wayne; Simon Pearce glass; Bardith plate. Page 32: Blue linen tray set by D. Porthault; ivory salt and pepper set from J. Garvin Mecking. Page 50: Tray from William Wayne; glass salad bowl from Simon Pearce. Page 53: Antique platter from More and More Antiques; Bardith cakestand; napkin from D. Porthault. Page 81: Louis XVI painted oval-backed reproduction armchair and fabric on chair by Brunschwig & Fils. Page 93: Napkins by D. Porthault; glasses and flatware by Williams-Sonoma; Simon Pearce basket. Page 128: Bardith plate. Page 135: White linen napkin from D. Porthault; ivory and silver pepper grinder from J. Garvin Mecking. Page 195: Merian bowl and Lowestoft Pink tureen by Mottahedeh. Page 202: Chair, chair fabric, and D'Artagnan woven floral stripe fabric on wall from Brunschwig & Fils; console from More and More Antiques; Bardith bowl and green cake plate, Frederick P. Victoria & Son Inc.; Lowestoft Pink round platter from Mottahedeh; champagne glasses from Williams-Sonoma.

This book, of course, is for Madam

Acknowledgments

It took a lot of help from a lot of people to make this book. Thanks go especially to Caroline and John Kennedy, who kept urging me to write a cookbook and kept supporting me while I did it.

And to Nancy Tuckerman, who figured out how to make it happen.

To Ed Schlossberg, my biggest supporter. And to Rose, Tatiana, and Jack Schlossberg, and Carolyn Bessette, who always brag about me. And for all their encouragement and many kindnesses, thanks to Marie Amaral; Bea and Joe Costa; Sibylle, Jean-Paul, Constance, Elie, and Victoria Denfert Rochereau; Yvette Eastman; Lisa Greenberg; Robert Hummelsbach; Katherine Hourigan; Jennifer Josephy; Elaine Kennelly; William Ivey Long; Kate Medina; Lee Nasso; Joan Pagano; Efigénio Pinheiro; Anthony and Carole Radziwill; Svenja Soldovieri; Maurice Templesman, Nicole Seligman, and Nana, Sheriff, Paula, and Daniel Wolff.

To Romulo Yanes (photographer), Lori Walther (food stylist), and Susan Victoria (stylist) for the beautiful food photographs and the fun of watching them being prepared.

To everyone at Scribner and Simon & Schuster who was always gracious and patient and cheerful, especially Susan Moldow, Roz Lippel, Beth Wareham, Mary Sexton, John Fontana, Blythe Grossberg, and Lisa Drew.

And finally to New York's most raffiné agent, Barney Karpfinger.

Contents

Before you start making any of these recipes, you should understand something. When I'm figuring out how much to make, I always allow for each person to have a first serving then that the dish will go around again and at least half the people will take a second, smaller serving. So if I say a dish serves six, remember that includes some second helpings and it could serve eight or nine if everyone only had one.

FOREWORD

When I was eight years old and my sister was eleven, we were introduced to our new governess while staying at my grandmother's house during the summer. Her name was Marta, and I was told that she didn't speak English. That made me immediately suspicious because I'd heard this before about the other bilingual au pairs who had helped care for us. It was part of my mother's tireless effort to get my sister and me to learn French. But after a few weeks they'd break down, and within a year or two, we'd say a tearful good-bye (in English) and wait for the next one to appear.

Marta broke down and started speaking English after about twenty-four hours, and thirty years later she is still part of our family. During those years her role evolved, and she settled in as an exquisite cook after we grew too old to be nannied. It's a bit surprising that Marta, who was always laconic about her recipes, should now have written a cookbook. Her dishes always seemed to just happen. Years ago, when I asked her how she made her singularly delicious scrambled eggs, she would say only, "I beat them up." The secret to preparing a temperamental Hollandaise sauce? "Don't look at her—if you do she will just turn."

This is something more than a cookbook, as you will see, and Marta found healing in revisiting the family moments described within. May you enjoy her creations as much as we did.

JOHN F. KENNEDY, JR.

Marta – Bravo et

Merci!

Everyone said it was the best dinner ever in New York!!

Je t'embrasse

Merci encore

XO J

How I Came to Be the Cook for Jacqueline Kennedy Onassis

I came from a little town in Italy—about four hundred people. I wanted to be an actress, but my mother didn't want me to leave home because I was very young. So I stayed and finished school. But I always dreamed of traveling. Starting when I was seven or eight, I wanted to explore, and the only thing that stopped me was how would I find my way home?

Finally, I went to Venice, where my sister was working for a shipping company. Through a friend of hers I was offered a job in the home of a French diplomatic family: Monsieur and Madame Gaussen and their five children—four boys and they had just had a girl. I loved kids and had always liked to be with them, and I thought this was a good chance for me to learn French, so I took the job. The boys had their own French governess, and I was engaged to look after the new baby, Sibylle. I had her from scratch and I not only liked being her nanny, and later her governess, I loved her as though she was my own.

At that time, M. Gaussen was attached to the French Embassy in Venice. While I was living there with them, I was able to fulfill my duties and also to study acting. The Gaussens treated me like a member of the family. Then, at the end of

M. Gaussen's tenure in Venice, the family moved to Paris and took me with them. This made me very happy.

Even before we left for Paris, the boys' French governess, Mademoiselle Escribe, had started teaching me not only how to speak French but also the rules of etiquette. I was included in the same classes as the boys. She was very strict. We weren't permitted to yawn in her presence. But the French I learned from her is very grammatical, very good. Now French has actually become my first language. Of course, I'm still Italian and speak it. But when I read or write it now it's a greater effort for me than French.

I was about eighteen when I first came to the Gaussens and was used to an unrestrained, freewheeling country environment. We lived in a palace in Venice, and I ran from room to room like an unleashed puppy. Often I'd be pushing a big old family crib on wheels along the passageways as I ran. They still talk about it. I always felt like running, but I was told I had to learn to walk, like a lady. That is still not natural for me.

In Paris I started to go to school, to finish my education. Until that time I had only studied theater, and I needed other training in case I wanted to do something different later, if my career as an actress didn't work out. I played lots of theater with the children, but I also went to La Sorbonne and got my diploma in French literature. Mlle Escribe had taught me such beautiful French that I gave the impression of knowing more than I really did. This made me study extra hard because I was so afraid I would be found out.

We spent a year in Boston when M. Gaussen was at the Foreign Service Institute at Harvard. After that we returned to Paris for another four years. Then he was called to the French Embassy in Washington, and we lived there from 1960 to 1963. In Washington, at the embassy, there was a lot of social activity. You know, in the diplomatic corps you have to give a lot of cocktail and dinner parties. It's part of the job.

During that time I met Mrs. Auchincloss, the mother of Mrs. John F. Kennedy.

She wanted to "keep up" her French and was very much involved with a French theater group I belonged to, La Marotte.

We had a big repertoire, both classical and modern plays, and we gave performances twice a year. We auditioned, and whoever got the part, got the part. Whoever didn't get the part was supposed to work backstage. I loved it all. When you go onstage, you have stage fright for a few minutes, but then you feel quite comfortable and adore that clapping audience. This had been my dream since I was seven years old in Italy. Later, in New York I joined a group at Lenox Hill. We staged *Ten Little Indians.* This was in English, so I had a tough time, but it was fun.

Here I am in the south of France, holding Pucci. Sibylle is looking at us from inside the house.

I sensed Mrs. Auchincloss was fond of me, but I didn't suspect that she had a plan and thought I would be the ideal person to work for her daughter and be a companion to her grandchildren. But gradually I figured it out from her questions about the Gaussen family. "How old are the children now?" "Will you stay with the family?" I always told her yes, I would stay. That was my home. Where else would I go? And why?

Sibylle was fourteen or fifteen by then, and she and her brothers were in school, so my work had shifted to organizing and helping with the many cocktail and dinner parties, all the entertaining the family was expected to do because of their position. I wasn't cooking at all. We had a very good cook. But I was doing the organizing with Mme Gaussen. At the party we each took half the guests, then we'd engage them in conversation and keep them entertained.

When we returned to Paris, I got a letter asking me if I would consider coming to work for the Kennedys. It was hard for them to reach me because we moved so often, but nonetheless we began an extended correspondence. I was torn. One part of me wanted to accept the Kennedy offer, and I was flattered to have been chosen. But the rest of me clung to the Gaussens. I loved the family and my good life with them. I didn't have to change. And, I reasoned, not only were the Kennedys strangers to me—except for what I read about them—they lived in New York, and I was frightened by New York based on the one weekend I had spent there.

But I didn't say no outright, and our correspondence continued. Mrs. Kennedy said she would be in England in February and suggested that we meet. I answered that I would be glad to meet her. Because maybe we wouldn't like each other. You know, it's a chemistry.

Then, a month after that letter, Mrs. Kennedy got married to Mr. Onassis, and we decided we would leave things the way they were. It would be too much for the children to change governesses at the same time they were trying to get used to their mother's new marriage and the new household.

So we never met in England, but we met in Paris. One day a chauffeur rang our bell and said that Mr. Onassis was in Paris and would I please meet him. I persuaded myself I should at least listen to what he had to say.

So I went to see him, and we talked for two hours. He was a very friendly, likable man. Mr. Onassis ended by saying OK, I'm going to tell my wife that we met, and I like you, so we're going to get in touch with you. I had agreed to take the job if everything worked out.

Well, that made me even more nervous. I had been protected all my life, because Sibylle's mother was like my mother. Every move I made, she was there directing me and telling me what to do and watching out for me. Suddenly I was going to find myself on my own! I thought, what am I going to do? I don't know how to do anything on my own.

And then the Onassises did get in touch with me. They called me up and asked if I could meet them in Greece.

I talked this over with my French "mother," Mme Gaussen. She was most supportive and convinced me it was time to try my wings, to try something new. But, she said, nobody was making me go and I didn't have to unless I wanted to. She also made it clear that if I didn't like it, I could come back home, that their home was mine too. And she explained that for her when I left, it would be as if she were sending a daughter to college. But I still felt uneasy—almost desperate—about leaving them.

Then we began making fun of the whole thing. The family laughed because I wanted to take Pucci, my long-haired dachshund, with me. They worked it out; "You can't go to work with a dog. If you like the job and plan to stay, we'll send you the dog. But you cannot just arrive with him."

Then, in July, instead of my going to Greece, Mrs. Onassis came to Paris. She sent me a little note saying she hoped that I would come and see her. We spent an hour together, and she hired me then and there. A little while later Mrs. Onassis's secretary, Miss Tuckerman, wrote to me saying how enthusiastic Mrs. Onassis was about seeing me, that she was waiting for my arrival.

I spent the rest of the summer of 1969 with the Gaussens in Barcelona. Then, in September, with really a big sadness on my heart, I said good-bye to everybody. I remember we had a Spanish girl who was working for us at the time who changed the sheets every Saturday and I was leaving on a Sunday and on Saturday I went to her and said, "Paquita, don't change my sheets. I am going to sleep on them one night, but don't change them because by next weekend I'm going to be back." I was determined. I was going. And I was coming back. Because I'd promised I'd go, I would go. So they couldn't say I didn't keep my word. But then I wouldn't like it and I was going to come back. I was completely determined about that.

This is how Caroline and John looked when we first met. I did not *bake that cake for John. Charlie, the butler, had a friend with the hobby of baking elaborate cakes, and he liked to make them for the children.*

Mrs. Onassis was in Greece, and I was to join the children in Newport, Rhode Island, where they were staying with their grandmother, Mrs. Auchincloss. So I flew to New York. Then I flew from New York to Newport in a storm, in a small flimsy plane. The storm had delayed us, so I didn't arrive until almost ten in the evening. I was met by Mr. Walsh, the head of our Secret Service detail, who drove me to Hammersmith Farm.

After greeting me, Mrs. Auchincloss said, "The children can't wait to see you, but John fell asleep. Caroline is still up. I'll take you to meet her." When we got to Caroline's bedroom there were two beds. Caroline had a friend staying with her. When I first looked at the two girls, I didn't know which one was which, and I looked at them and thought, "I hope it's that one." I'll never forget that. And that one was Caroline. So I felt I liked her the first minute I saw her.

The children—who were eleven and eight by then—and I adjusted to each other easily, with no problems. We stayed in Newport for a couple of weeks, until school started and we did lots of things together: bicycle riding, going to the beach, and playing all kinds of outdoor games. Back in New York, I had my first experience with paparazzi—which was both annoying and frightening—when I took John for his first day at Collegiate. The next day there was a picture of us on the front page of the *Daily News* and other papers all over the world. I couldn't believe it. Everyone saw it. I even got a letter from the director of my French theater group congratulating me for being the first member of La Marotte to make the front page.

We were in New York for the school week. I took the children not only to school but also to whatever they were doing after, like playing tennis in Central Park. We went back to Newport for the weekends.

When Mrs. Onassis returned from Greece a few weeks later, we really started to live with each other, adjust to each other, to know each other. That first year on weekends Mr. Onassis's Lear jet would take us to Puerto Rico, where the *Christina* picked us up, and then we'd cruise for two or three days in the Caribbean. Then the plane would take us back to New York, and the kids would go to school on Monday. There were also frequent, longer trips to Greece on vacations.

The picture that made front pages all over the world, of me taking John for his first day at Collegiate.

It was a fantastic, different life I hadn't even known existed. My memories of it now are like dreams.

That was when the name "Madam" was settled on. When I was with the Gaussens I called the parents Monsieur and Madame, which is the polite, formal,

This dress had been Madam's. After she gave it to me, I wore it for years because I loved the little airplane print. I still have the scarf.

European way. I came to the United States without much English, but, naturally, wanting to be correct.

So I began calling Mrs. Onassis Madam because that sounded to me like the American translation of Madame.

One day Mrs. Onassis asked me, Do you know what a madam is? I told her it was the English name for the mistress of the house. She then explained that it really wasn't; that in English the word had a somewhat risqué meaning. And she told me what it meant.

I began to apologize, but she stopped me and laughed and told me not to stop using the title because it was so cute.

Some years later Caroline went to boarding school. John was in his school most of the day, and I didn't have enough to keep me busy. I did a lot of volunteer work, but I still had time. That's when I got interested in cooking.

It started on the *Christina.* There aren't many things to do on a boat, so I'd go into the kitchen and watch the cooking. The chefs would teach me. I used to watch the chefs prepare Greek food for the crew and whoever else wanted it, and French food for the rest. It was all good food, well prepared. M. Clement, the head chef, had worked for Mr. Onassis for forty years and knew his preferences.

He was a real chef. I remember he tried to teach me how to make a Soufflé Arlequin, which is a soufflé of three colors: strawberry, chocolate, and vanilla. I wouldn't dare make it now.

I had never done any real cooking before. My sisters were good cooks, but my mother never thought I could do it. The only thing she let me do was peel potatoes, and then she thought I took off more than peel and shrank the potatoes too much. Later I always lived in houses where there was a cook.

When he came to New York the first year, Mr. Onassis was not happy with the cooks Mrs. Onassis had there. Clement came to New York with us very little. He was married and his post was in Monte Carlo, where he had a wife and kids, or on the boat when the boat was cruising. He came to New York and stayed a month or two, but then he went back. He didn't like New York.

By the time John was ready to go to boarding school, because of all my watching, I had started to learn to cook the foods Mr. and Mrs. Onassis liked. I had done a little cooking for Caroline and John and occasionally for Mr. and Mrs. Onassis when they joined us on weekends in New Jersey. I loved to surprise them. And then one day in 1974 they asked me how would I like to be the cook. I liked to cook, I told them, so I'd try it and we'd see. I never took over in Europe. There were chefs there. But I became the cook in the New York apartment.

The kids were in school, and even with my volunteer work and all the little things I was doing, I had plenty of time to make dinner. In fact, it kept me busy. At lunch nobody was there. Breakfast is nothing. So it was just dinner.

This picture of me was really taken my first year with the family when we visited Egypt. But looking at it now, I sort of think of it as a photograph of my arrival in Caroline's and John's lives.

After Mr. Onassis died, the food changed. We ate lighter, leaner food, less elaborate meals. Mrs. Onassis liked what I was cooking. John, when he was going to be home for dinner, used to call me first and ask what I was making. He'd always say, "I don't want to eat any of your diet food." Of course, I made him the kind of food he liked.

On Martha's Vineyard there was more cooking because there were three meals and houseguests who would want more extensive breakfasts, with eggs and stuff like that. And then a different lunch. If Madam was by herself, she'd have a slice of cold chicken, some cottage cheese, and tomatoes every day.

When guests were there, we had tomato and ricotta pies or zucchini vegetable pies. Or frittata or vegetable chowders. It depended on the weather a little. If it was cool, we'd have soup and more chowders. And then dinners also had to be a little fancier, with a dessert. If she was alone, Madam loved plain fruit, but if you have guests you have to make a dessert.

But most of the time it was just Madam and me on Martha's Vineyard, very nice and free and easy. We had no obligations. She was living her life; I, mine. Sometimes she worried that I'd get bored, but I reassured her that I had my life with my friends, my car, the beach anytime I wanted. And the beautiful island.

Follow-up Note

People who have read this have asked what finally happened to my dog. I thought I would really miss little Pucci when I left him behind with Sibylle, but a few years later Mr. Onassis gave me a note with a picture of Pucci drawn by Madam, who liked to draw and did wonderful little sketches. The note said that anytime I wanted my dog, he would have him picked up for me in Paris. But I decided Sibylle needed him more than I did. I missed Sibylle very much, and we talked and wrote all the time, but now, even though they weren't the same, I had a whole new family. I was very happy with them. Sibylle only had the dog as a souvenir of me, so I left him.

Then two years after I left them, my French family came to the consulate in New York so I could see them and Pucci all the time. Sometimes he stayed with me and sometimes with them. When they left New York for another posting, he was too old to enjoy traveling, so they left him with me. Finally, when he got really old, I found him a nice place on Long Island where he could be outdoors with other animals and he lived another few years.

This is Madam posing proudly with the Irish spaniels Shannon and Whiskey. Shannon had been given to the President when he visited Ireland. Whiskey was his son.

1

JANUARY

Winter Dinner after Sledding in Central Park

✻

When I first came, we almost never spent winter weekends in the city. That's what the New Jersey house was for. We went there if we weren't going somewhere on the *Christina.* That year the boat was moored in the United States, and Mr. Onassis liked to spend time on the boat, with us flying in. That way we could go someplace interesting and beautiful and warm and still have privacy.

In the summer we were never in New York. When John and Caroline were young, we were in Greece. Later we went to Hyannis—until 1980, when the house on Martha's Vineyard was built. When we were going to Greece, we would come back in August and go to Hyannis until September. Then we'd have to come back to New York because school was starting. On Martha's Vineyard or in Hyannis or in Greece, there was always swimming, sailing, water skiing, running on the beach. There were other sports the children did with their cousins, like football or touchball or baseball.

On winter weekends we went skiing a lot, at Hunter Mountain, which is near, in upstate New York. We went Friday and came back Sunday night. I took John more than Caroline. She was three years older so she went to boarding school three years sooner. I still had her on vacations, but I had more of him.

I remember John and I went to France one year to ski with the Kennedys and Mrs. Lawford. And then another year the family went all together to Switzerland except for Mr. Onassis, who couldn't come. They all skied very well. They still ski. John goes very often. Caroline started to take her girls over spring break when they were about to be nine and seven. They're starting good and early.

After a while Caroline and John wanted to stay in the city on weekends during the school year for birthday parties or whatever, and we began having playtime in New York. On weekends we went to the park, and after school I'd pick the children up around three o'clock and take them to the park to play for an hour or so. The whole family has a lot of energy, so we were always out doing things.

We never went ice skating. Maybe roller skates, but I don't remember. We may have once or twice, but it was not something we did regularly. We went sledding on that hill behind the Metropolitan Museum. Caroline and John loved that. Sometimes the cousins who lived nearby would come too, or sometimes their friends.

In September, October, until the cold came, maybe until Thanksgiving, we went once a week to Central Park so the kids could play tennis; they had a teacher named Mr. Fenton, I remember. We would walk all the way up to the tennis courts followed by the Secret Service. There were lots of them because each child had one. I think they changed every eight hours, so we always had two at a time. The chief, Mr. Walsh, who had met me in Newport, was in charge of them all. We're still in touch with him. He lives in Boston now, but he calls me all the time.

When we came back home we always had some sort of a teatime. Especially with children, you give them a snack or you give them tea. When it was cold outside, we had hot chocolate with whipped cream and marshmallows. Both marshmallows and whipped cream in the same cup. Children love that. More is mooshy. More is sloppy. It had to look generous.

And always CINNAMON TOAST. I always remember John and Caroline and cinnamon toast around teatime.

I made it with toasting bread—thin-sliced good bread like Pepperidge Farm or Arnold—that you toast first and then you put some butter on it and then you sprinkle it with one part cinnamon and three of sugar. Then you put it under the broiler until it starts to bubble. And you have to eat it hot.

This with hot chocolate or sometimes Toll House cookies.

That would keep them until dinner.

When I started working on this book, I asked Caroline and John what their favorite foods had been. Caroline said creamed chicken with rice and peas, and John remembered loving chipped beef on toast for lunch. For both of those I made a béchamel sauce and mixed the chicken or meat into it. They also liked chicken Kiev with kasha, roast beef with Yorkshire pudding, and beef stroganoff, and when they were very young, they liked veal scallops stuffed with sausage and cooked with carrots, then served with noodles. And when John was little, he loved sloppy Joes. Even before I really knew how to cook, I made them for him. I put chopped meat and onions on a hamburger bun, then poured sauce over it all. I guess in those days I probably used Ragú. I told John that was not going to go into this book.

These were not the kinds of food Madam liked to eat. She preferred what John called her "diet food," light, good food. But Madam would eat creamed chicken or beef stroganoff because they were what her children wanted and her children were everything to her. And meals were a time for the family to be together. Nancy Tuckerman told me that before I came, Mrs. Kennedy used to have a big map of the world hanging in the dining room, and she would sit with the children while they ate and show them, on the map, the places their father had traveled when he was president.

The two meals here are from later, when I was cooking. This is the food Madam liked on a cold night. There would be a fire in the dining room, which was cozy. And the table looked cheerful, covered with a flowered chintz cloth. Madam had those in several colors, and she would tell me to use the brown or the pink or whatever. There was a bottom cloth that went to the floor and stayed on all the time, and then another cloth on top of that. The top cloth was the same fabric but didn't come down as far; it just covered the top of the table and hung down a little. There were two or three of the top cloths in each pattern, so after a meal the top cloth, which was the only one that might have gotten dirty, could be taken off and laundered and a new one put on. The bottom cloth never got dirty, so it stayed.

And there were always candles, red or ivory or blue, mostly the square Cape Cod candles. We generally used some big candlesticks that I think might have been a wedding present when Madam married John Kennedy. I never really knew what they were until I read a description in the auction catalog that said they were Napoleon III, made of ormolu and patinaed brass. Madam always liked beautiful things around her. They didn't have to be fancy, but she cared about details. For instance, she didn't like the look of big vegetables. So for a dish like Scallops Baked with a Julienne of Vegetables, if I could only find big vegetables, I had to cut them up.

Rolled Stuffed Loin of Lamb

Serves 4

3–4-pound loin of lamb
Salt and pepper
½ cup chopped parsley
1 Tablespoon fresh rosemary leaves
3 cloves garlic, peeled

Preheat the oven to 375°.

You can ask your butcher to butterfly the lamb or do it yourself. If you do it, it means slitting it lengthwise the whole length of the loin but not all the way through. Place the lamb, cut side up, on a horizontal surface, open it like a book, and flatten it out as much as possible, then season the inside with salt and pepper.

In a small food processor, grind together the parsley, rosemary, and garlic until they are a very fine mince. Spread this down the center of the loin, then very carefully roll up the loin, starting at one long side. This is seasoning more than filling, to give a taste to the lamb. Try to keep it in place. Tie the roll every few inches with kitchen string to help it hold its shape.

On top of the stove, but in a roasting pan, brown the lamb on all sides. This will take about 5 minutes. Then place the browned meat in the oven and roast for 20 minutes. This will make a nice rare, pink roast.

Remove from the oven and keep the lamb warm for 10 minutes before removing the strings and serving.

Jean Claude's Baked Three-Bean Dish

This dish, which I was taught by Jean Claude Nedelec of Glorious Food, I always served with the rolled lamb. It's a variation on the classic lamb with beans and, I think, even better.

8 ounces (1 cup) each dried kidney beans, flageolets, and cannellini
3 bay leaves
1 shallot, minced very finely
3 cloves garlic, crushed
½ cup parsley, chopped
½ cup olive oil

Boil each kind of bean separately with a bay leaf until tender. Strain, remove the bay leaves, and combine the beans in one large flat baking dish.

Preheat the oven to 350°.

Stir the minced shallot, garlic, and parsley into the beans. Begin drizzling the olive oil over the top. You may not need the whole amount. You want all the beans to be coated lightly but not swimming in oil.

(continued on next page)

Bake for 20 minutes or until the beans are tender. This will depend on the beans, but begin poking with a fork after about 15 minutes. When the beans are cooked, the shallot and garlic should disappear and the parsley just be little green flecks.

Tomates à la Provençale

4 medium or 8 small tomatoes
3 cloves garlic
½ cup minced parsley
¼ cup plain dry bread crumbs
Salt and pepper

Cut the tomatoes in half around the hemisphere. Being careful to keep the skin intact, scoop the pulp out into a bowl. Mince the garlic, then add it, the parsley, and the bread crumbs to the pulp. Taste and correct seasoning, then return the mixture into the hollowed-out skins.

Arrange the tomatoes in a lightly oiled baking dish and place under a preheated broiler for anywhere from 5 to 15 minutes. They are ready when the skins retain their shape and the filling is lightly browned.

Poached Red Plums

Serves 4 to 6

1 cup sugar
Zest, the orange part of the rind, of 2 oranges, julienned
1½ pounds (10 to 12) red plums

In a saucepan large enough to hold all the plums submerged in syrup, stir the sugar into two cups of water and bring to a boil. Lower the heat, add the zest, and simmer for 5 minutes.

Prick each plum twice with the tines of a fork, then place them carefully in the syrup. Cover and let simmer to poach for 5 minutes.

Let the plums cool in the syrup, then slip off their skins, which should be easy to do. Return the skinned plums to the syrup and let them steep until you are ready to serve. These can be served at room temperature or chilled.

I used to serve these in a wonderful gold vermeil bowl that reflected the color of the plums beautifully.

Scallops Baked with a Julienne of Vegetables

Serves 4 as a main course, 8 as an appetizer

1 pound (4 or 5 medium) plum tomatoes
2 Tablespoons minced parsley
1 Tablespoon minced basil
1 clove garlic, minced
2½ Tablespoons unsalted butter, divided
¼ cup julienned celery
¼ cup julienned carrots
¼ cup julienned white turnips
¼ cup julienned leek (white part only)
Salt and pepper
1 pound bay scallops
Additional parsley for garnish

(continued on page 33)

Preheat the oven to very hot, 450°.

Start by preparing the tomatoes. Bring a saucepan of water to a boil and lower the tomatoes in, one at a time, for no more than 5 seconds. When the tomatoes are removed from the water, you should be able to slip the skins off. Then squeeze the seeds out and chop the pulp that remains. You should have about 1½ cups. Put it into a small bowl.

Add the minced parsley, basil, and garlic.

Melt 2 tablespoons butter in a saucepan. Add the julienned celery, carrots, turnips, and leek. Before you julienne the vegetables make sure you wash the leek very carefully. They hold soil. Each bit of the julienne should be about 2 inches long and very, very thin.

Season with salt and pepper, then cover the pan. Over low heat sweat the vegetables for about 5 minutes or until they are soft.

While they are sweating, rinse the scallops and pat them dry.

I cooked and served this dish in scallop shells I got in France, but if you don't have them, you can use 4 small (3-inch) ramekins, the kind individual crèmes brûlées are often served in.

If you are making this dish for 4, arrange one-eighth of the vegetables in the bottom of each of whatever four containers you have chosen. Cover each with one-eighth of the tomato mixture, then arrange a quarter of the scallops over that. Season with salt and pepper, then cover with another one-eighth of the vegetables. Top everything with the last eighth of the tomato mixture.

Place the containers on a baking sheet or jelly roll pan and bake in the middle of the oven for about 5 minutes. This is ready when the liquid is bubbling and the scallops, if you can see them, have become opaque.

Carefully pour the liquid out of each shell or ramekin, then replace it on the baking sheet. Top each with a quarter of the remaining ½ tablespoon butter.

Return to the oven and bake for another 5 minutes or until the butter is bubbling.

Transfer the ramekins onto individual serving plates, fluff the contents with a fork, then garnish each with a little chopped parsley.

Coeur à la Crème

Serves 4 to 6

You will need a special heart-shaped mold to make this, but they are available at any good cookware store. They are made of metal or porcelain, with holes for drainage. I make this in one larger mold, but they also come in a size for individual portions. You will also need some cheesecloth which is easy to find at any hardware store.

8 ounces cream cheese
½ cup confectioners' sugar
½ vanilla bean
2 cups heavy cream

SAUCE

1 (10-ounce) package frozen raspberries
½ cup red currant jelly
1 Tablespoon Framboise (a raspberry-flavored liqueur)
1 pint fresh strawberries

Beat the cream cheese with an electric mixer until it is light and fluffy. Slowly beat in the confectioners' sugar. Split the vanilla bean lengthwise and scrape the seeds into the mixture. Beat them in.

In another bowl, beat the cream until it holds its shape, but isn't stiff. Add the whipped cream to the cream cheese mixture and fold them together gently.

Cut a piece of cheesecloth large enough to line the mold and drape over the sides. Soak the cloth in ice water, then wring it out, and line the mold with it. Fill the lined mold with the cream cheese mixture. Fold the flaps of cheesecloth over the top of the dessert, place the mold on a plate to catch the drainage, and refrigerate until you are ready to serve.

To make the sauce, defrost the raspberries, then put them in a blender with the currant jelly and Framboise. Blend well, then pour the sauce through a strainer to remove the seeds.

To serve, unmold the heart onto a round serving platter and place strawberries all around the rim. Serve the sauce separately in a bowl with a ladle.

A family holiday dinner, with Madam crowded but happy between Ed and her niece, Alexandra Rutherford.

2
FEBRUARY

Lunch on a Tray with One Friend

Sometimes when Madam had one friend coming for lunch, she would want to eat in the library on trays. In winter it was more cozy with the fire. If there were more than two people, Madam always ate in the dining room. For family she always liked only one table, and not a big one, no matter how many people there were. She wanted everybody at the same table even if we had to crowd in. The most we had was seventeen, I think, one Christmas. Sometimes, like at Christmas, we had to squeeze in so tight we could barely move our arms up to eat. You really had to eat properly because there was no room for your elbows. But it didn't matter because it was all family.

If there was a big party, not for family, but when we had a dinner party for a lot of guests, we took out the regular table and brought in two or three round tables for six or eight. There were maybe two or three times during my time we had fifteen or sixteen guests. This would be for an occasion like maybe the opening of the ballet. People coming for that sort of dinner wouldn't want to sit squeezed together the way the family did.

Then we didn't use our own chairs because they were quite substantial. Instead, we rented smaller gold chairs but we had our own cushions to put on them so they looked a little nicer.

The tables usually came with damask cloths to fit them, so we used those, and I always did the flowers and the centerpieces anyway. We had lots of china because Madam liked a beautiful table, so we just decided which dishes to use for what. Nothing was in sets. All the dishes on the table matched each other, but not the ones for the other courses. We would use the pink for the first course, the green for the main course, and so on. The silver was the same we always used, only if there were guests it was probably newly polished.

If Madam was having lunch with one friend in the library, I always had everything already out on the trays so they wouldn't be interrupted. I prepared something like chicken salad or crab salad (Madam didn't care so much for shrimp) or some kind of vegetable-based salad. Also in the summer Madam liked Mussel Salad. And there was always pita bread which was split, then each round cut in half, lightly buttered and toasted under the grill, then sprinkled with dill. Fresh is best, but you can use dried. We had that anyway with almost every meal. Sometimes I found different sizes of pita so I could grill the small rounds without splitting them. The bread was always in a basket on the table.

For dessert I would have something that could sit on the tray and not spoil. If I could find them, I'd have big strawberries, hulled, or good cherries or, in the summer, cut-up peaches and blueberries.

These lunches were mostly for when Madam wanted to talk quietly with one friend. Hillary Clinton had one of those lunches, although she also came for dinner with others. And I remember lunches with Janie Hitchcock, Margot Fonteyn, Jayne Wrightsman, and of course, Madam's mother.

There were more casual lunches for two on the Vineyard, because during the winter Madam was going to work and didn't usually come home for lunch. And the Vineyard was more casual anyway. No matter how many were eating, lunch was always outside if the weather was good. For one or two it was on the porch under the umbrella, and we could seat more at the table outside the pantry. I would make simple lunches from what was fresh and good. I used those ingredients for dinners too, but at dinner I would also take the seasonal fruit, which Madam loved, and make it into desserts like Strawberry Mousse or Pear

Sorbet. Madam liked light fruit desserts anytime. Even in winter at the end of a heavier meal, she preferred them.

When Diana Vreeland came for dinner, she always asked Madam if I could make Shepherd's Pie for her because she thought I made a really good one. Maybe it was because other people didn't do mashed potatoes the way I did. That is a heavy dish with potatoes and meat, so I would serve it with a light first course—a soup or some vegetable dish like artichoke hearts—and then a light dessert.

Even when there were six or eight guests—Madam didn't like more than that for dinner—she used to bring them into the kitchen. She was so proud of me and wanted to show me off. That was one of the ways Madam was special. Like the little notes she slipped under my door almost every night. She was very appreciative of any small thing you did for her. And that made you try even harder to do a little more. I was glad she was proud of me, but I would say to her, "Not to the kitchen; I'm not presentable." Sometimes she would bring them in while I was trying to get dinner ready and I really wanted to concentrate. I almost never cooked anything ahead. I might prepare, but usually I didn't start the cooking until about half an hour before everyone was going to sit down. I'd have the first course ready, then cook the main course while that was being eaten and get the salad ready during the main course and the dessert during the salad. It all went pretty fast, because Madam didn't like to spend too much time sitting at the table.

One time she brought in Placido Domingo while I was cooking, and although I was pleased to meet him, the time was not convenient. Afterward I told Madam I was happy she wanted to show me off, but I was a little busy during the meal. And anyway, I said, if she really wanted to impress me she should introduce me to Pavarotti, who is Italian. Domingo is a Spaniard.

Watercress Soup

Serves 6

6 Tablespoons (3/4 stick) butter

4 bunches scallions (white part only), cut into 1/4-inch-thick slices

5 bunches watercress

6 red potatoes, thinly sliced

5 cups chicken stock (see page 132)

Salt and pepper

1 cup heavy cream

Melt the butter in a 2-quart saucepan. Add the slices of scallions, cover, and cook slowly until they are soft, about 15 minutes.

Add the watercress and potatoes, stir well, and cook, uncovered, for 10 more minutes. Add the chicken stock, cover, and cook for another 45 minutes.

Add salt and pepper to taste, then let cool. Puree the cool soup in a food processor, then return it to the pot. Stir in the cream and reheat, but be careful not to let the soup boil or the cream could curdle.

Mussel Salad

Serves 4

MUSSELS

1 1/2 quarts mussels in their shells

1/4 cup fish stock (recipe follows)

2 Tablespoons dry white wine

Half of the white part of a leek

1 shallot, minced

Put 4 individual serving plates into the refrigerator to chill.

Scrub the mussels well. Place them in a large saucepan with the rest of ingredients. Cover, bring to a boil, and boil 5 minutes or until all the shells open.

Remove the mussels, then strain and reserve the liquid they cooked in. Take all the mussels out of their shells except for 4, which will be for decoration. Discard any that haven't opened.

SAUCE

1 teaspoon olive oil
½ shallot, finely minced
1 teaspoon crème fraîche (see page 99)
A pinch of saffron
Reserved mussel cooking liquid

In a small saucepan, heat the olive oil. Add the shallot, crème fraîche, saffron, and about ⅔ of a cup of the reserved cooking liquid. Bring to a boil, boil for about 1 minute, then remove from the heat and add the mussels. Stir and let cool.

SALAD

2 hearts of Bibb lettuce, plus a few perfect extra leaves
Lemon
2 small stalks celery, cut into 2-inch-long julienne strips
1 tomato, peeled, seeded, and diced
½ teaspoon coarsely chopped fresh tarragon

Arrange the lettuce hearts and leaves on the chilled serving plates. Squeeze a little lemon juice over the lettuce, then top with the mussels. Spoon just a little of the sauce over the mussels.

Decorate each plate with the julienned celery, the diced tomato, the chopped tarragon, and one of the mussels left in its shell.

Fish Stock

Makes 3 to 4 quarts

5 pounds assorted fish pieces, including heads, tails, and spines. (Use parts of any white fish. Avoid using anything from oily fish such as blues or salmon. You can either save these pieces yourself in your freezer or do it the easier way and ask your fish man for them. If he charges you at all, it won't be much.)
2 onions, peeled and chopped
3 stalks celery with leaves, chopped
3 unpeeled carrots with tops, cut into medium slices
5 sprigs fresh thyme or 2 Tablespoons dried
2 bay leaves
20 black peppercorns
6 sprigs parsley
2 cups dry white wine

Check to make sure the gills have been removed from all fish heads. Rinse all the fish pieces under cold running water.

Put the rinsed fish in a large kettle or stockpot with all the rest of the ingredients and enough cold water to cover. Bring to a boil, then lower the heat so it is simmering. Cover and simmer for 35 minutes, skimming the top once or twice.

Rinse a large piece of cheesecloth and wring it out. Use the damp cheesecloth, doubled, to line a large strainer. Place the strainer over a capacious clean pot and ladle the fish stock into it. Don't press the juices out of the bones and vegetables; first let them sit in the strainer for 10 minutes until all the liquid drips out, then discard. Let the stock cool, then refrigerate.

This will last in the refrigerator for a day or two, or freeze in pint or quart containers to use when you need it.

Salade d'Haricots Verts

Serves 6 to 8 as an appetizer

It is important that this salad be served at room temperature. Chilling dulls the delicacy of its flavors.

1½ pounds fresh green beans, the smallest you can find
8 ounces pâté de foie gras
⅓ cup light olive oil (not first press which has too strong a taste)
2 Tablespoons raspberry vinegar
Salt and pepper
3 shallots, minced
1 teaspoon fresh chervil or 2 Tablespoons parsley—either should be finely chopped

Bring 3 quarts of water to a rolling boil. Meanwhile, trim the beans. Drop the beans in the rapidly boiling water and cook for about 8 minutes. The beans must retain their crispness. Drain and cool just slightly.

Cut the pâté into matchstick-sized pieces, the same size as the beans.

Gently, so nothing breaks, mix the beans and pâté together.

Blend the oil, vinegar, salt, and pepper and pour it over the salad. Add the shallots, toss, and sprinkle with chopped chervil or parsley.

TABBOULEH

Serves 4 to 6

½ cup bulgur
2 medium tomatoes
1 shallot
2 Tablespoons chopped fresh mint
Juice of half a lemon
2 Tablespoons olive oil
Salt and pepper

In a medium-sized heatproof bowl, pour 2 cups of boiling water over the bulgur. Let stand for 1 hour. Chop the tomatoes and the shallot and stir them together in a small bowl. Stir in the chopped mint. (Sometimes I also use cucumber, peeled, seeded, and cut into small cubes.)

Pour the bulgur into a piece of cheesecloth and squeeze out any water that hasn't been absorbed. Put the bulgur in a serving bowl and add the chopped vegetables and mint, then the lemon juice, olive oil, salt, and pepper. Mix well and correct seasoning.

This goes great with cold lamb and grilled pita.

RATATOUILLE

Serves 8

2 sweet yellow peppers
2 sweet red peppers
2 green peppers
5 medium eggplants

6 ripe medium tomatoes
1 large onion
4 large cloves garlic
½ cup virgin olive oil
½ teaspoon fresh thyme leaves
1 cup chopped fresh basil leaves
¼ cup chopped Italian parsley
Salt and pepper

Seed the peppers and cut them into 1-inch squares. Using the three colors of peppers makes this dish more colorful, but you can use any combination or all of one so long as you use six peppers in all. Cut the eggplants into the same size cubes. Peel and seed the tomatoes and cube them too. Chop the onion and mince the garlic fine.

In a large heavy-bottomed saucepan (so nothing sticks), heat the olive oil. Add the onion and garlic, cover the pan, and over low heat let them sweat about 20 minutes or until they turn yellowish. They shouldn't brown.

Remove the lid and add the peppers, eggplants, tomatoes, thyme, basil, and parsley. Add salt and pepper to taste, stir well, then re-cover and cook over low heat, stirring frequently, for about 15 minutes.

Uncover the pan again, and raise the heat but not too high, and simmer another 25 to 30 minutes to reduce the juices and finish the cooking.

This can be served hot with meat, especially lamb, or at room temperature as a salad. It shouldn't be served cold because that makes the oil too solid.

If the weather was cool, Madam liked somewhat more substantial food for lunch, but then there would be no first course unless the lunch was a fancy one. For instance, when Hillary Clinton came for lunch in 1993, she ate OEUFS TOUPINEL. This is also the recipe

John chose when I asked him what favorite dish he wanted me to put in the book for him.

To make this for 6, you get big baking potatoes, one for each person, wash them, put them in a pan, and bake for 2 hours at 350°, until the flesh can be pierced easily with the point of a knife. While the potatoes are baking, make a simple Béchamel Sauce (see below) and mix some medium-sized pieces of cut-up ham into it. Also poach 6 eggs.

When the potatoes are baked, cut a slice off one of the long sides and, keeping the skins whole, scoop out the flesh and mash it.

Then you use each of those skins as a dish. Spoon in a little of the béchamel and on top of that put back some of the mashed potatoes. Save about ½ a cup after all the skins are filled. On top of the potato goes a poached egg. Then you season with salt and pepper. Finally you cover each one with a little of the reserved mashed potatoes and use a spoon to bring them up so that they come out over the skins a little. Make a crosshatch pattern on them with a fork and sprinkle with some grated Parmesan or Swiss cheese. Then they go back into the oven for a few minutes to reheat, and just before you serve them, you put them under the broiler so the tops get brown and crisp.

Béchamel Sauce

Makes 2 cups

2 Tablespoons butter
3 Tablespoons flour
2 cups milk, just at the boil

In a heavy 2-quart saucepan, melt the butter over low heat, then sprinkle the flour over it and slowly stir it in with a whisk. Don't let this roux brown or take on any color, but cook slowly, stirring, for about 3 minutes.

Turn the heat down until it is as low as you can get it and begin to add the hot milk a little at a time. Immediately begin stirring with a whisk. When the ingredients are blended and none of the roux is left unincorporated and you think the sauce is the right consistency (think sauce), stop adding the milk and cook for another 4 or 5 minutes to get rid of the raw flour taste, stirring and scraping the bottom of the pan all the time. As the sauce cooks it may thicken; if it does, add more milk. You may not need the whole 2 cups.

You can use other liquids to give this sauce a little more flavor. You might use chicken or meat stock instead of milk, depending on the dish it will be part of.

Tomato and Ricotta Tart

Serves 4 to 6

This is a lot of work to make, but it's worth it.

PASTRY SHELL

2 cups flour
Pinch of salt
3 Tablespoons shortening
8 Tablespoons (1 stick) unsalted butter, chilled and diced
1 egg, lightly beaten

Sift the flour and salt together into a bowl. Add the shortening and the butter and begin cutting them into the dry ingredients with a pastry blender or 2 forks. Finish making the mixture uniform with your fingertips, but try not to handle too much. The end product should resemble coarse cornmeal.

Add up to 4 tablespoons cold water and mix to form a rough dough. Shape the dough

(continued on next page)

into a ball and then remove it from the bowl and place on a floured surface. Use the heel of your hand and the weight of your body to smear out the dough, one small piece at a time. This ensures that the ingredients are completely incorporated.

Reshape the dough into a ball, wrap in waxed paper, and refrigerate for at least 2 hours.

When you are ready to bake, heat the oven to 450° and have ready an 8-inch flan ring on a cookie sheet.

Roll the chilled dough out on a floured surface. The rolled-out dough should be the right size to line the flan ring and a little more than ⅛ inch thick. Roll it up over the rolling pin and unroll it onto the ring. Let some dough hang over the sides of the ring, but carefully and neatly press it down around the inside. Prick the dough with a fork, cover with a piece of waxed paper, and weigh it down by spreading raw rice or dried beans over the paper.

Bake for 10 minutes at 450° then lower the heat to 250° and bake another 10 minutes. Remove from the oven, lift out the paper and the weights, and paint the inside of the shell with the beaten egg. Then run a sharp knife around the rim of the ring to cut off any excess pastry. Return to the oven and bake for a final 10 minutes.

Lift off the flan ring and let the pastry cool before filling.

FILLING

5 Tablespoons olive oil
1 medium onion, chopped
3 pounds (12 to 15, depending on size) ripe tomatoes, peeled, seeded, and diced
¼ cup chopped fresh basil
Salt and pepper

Heat the oil in a heavy skillet. Add the onion pieces and cook slowly until they are golden and soft. Add the tomato pulp and cook slowly for 1 hour or more, stirring from time to time, until all the moisture has evaporated and the mixture has reduced to a paste. Stir in the chopped basil and season with salt and pepper.

TOPPING

4 ripe tomatoes, about 3 inches at the widest diameter, peeled and sliced into ¼-inch-thick rounds
8 ounces ricotta, sliced thin and in the same shape as the tomato slices
2 Tablespoons butter, melted
Salt and pepper

To slice ricotta slide it from its container onto a piece of waxed paper. Wrap in 2 pieces of waxed paper and squeeze gently to make a log the same diameter as the tomatoes. Use a sharp knife to cut the cheese into ¼-inch-thick slices. This is not easy to do and you could substitute mozzarella, but the ricotta is tastier.

TO ASSEMBLE

Preheat the broiler.

Spread the filling evenly over the cooked pastry, then, starting at the outside rim, arrange alternating slices of tomato and cheese slices in concentric rings over the top. Use a spatula to pick up the cheese slices. Fill any gap left in the center with end slices of the tomatoes or a cherry tomato. Brush the surface with the melted butter and season with salt and pepper.

Place the tart under the broiler for about 5 minutes or until the cheese bubbles gently and takes on a bit of color.

Run a long, sharp knife under the pastry to make sure it comes loose from the cookie sheet. Then slide the tart onto a heated serving platter.

Serve hot or at room temperature.

Shepherd's Pie

Serves 6

4 cups chopped cooked lamb or roast beef (the meat must be rare)
2 large cloves garlic, chopped
1 large onion, chopped
1 teaspoon fresh rosemary leaves
8 Tablespoons (1 stick) butter, divided
3 Tablespoons flour
1 cup beef stock
Salt and pepper
4 cups mashed potatoes (see page 150)

Preheat oven to 350°.

Combine the lamb, garlic, onion, and rosemary and put them through a meat grinder twice. If you don't have a meat grinder, don't use a food processor because that doesn't give the right texture. Use a knife to chop the ingredients very fine, the way you would if you were making hash.

Melt 6 tablespoons of the butter in a large skillet and stir in the flour. Stirring constantly with a wooden spoon, cook for 5 minutes or until completely blended. Slowly add the stock, stirring as you add, and cook until thickened, about 5 minutes.

Add the chopped lamb mixture and stir to blend. Add salt and pepper to taste.

Spoon into a 2-quart oval ovenproof casserole. Spread the mashed potatoes over the top. They should be as even as possible and touch the rim of the casserole so that none of the meat mixture shows.

Use a fork to rake a design along the top, drawing the tines over the surface from one end to the other the long way. Dot with the remaining 2 tablespoons of butter.

Bake for 40 minutes or until the filling is bubbling hot and the potatoes are browned.

Frozen Lemon Soufflé

Serves 6

I used to make this soufflé often for parties, multiplying the recipe as needed to serve the number of guests. I always try to allow enough so that everyone can have two generous helpings and then there will some left over to go back into the freezer for snacking later.

The orphan egg whites can be frozen to be thawed and used later.

12 egg yolks
1¾ cups plus 2 teaspoons sugar, divided
¾ cup lemon juice
Grated zest of 1 lemon
½ cup heavy cream
6 egg whites

Select a deep-sided skillet or sauté pan that will comfortably hold a medium-sized heatproof bowl and allow room for water to come up the sides of the bowl on the outside. After testing, remove and dry the bowl and bring the water in the skillet to a boil.

Beat the 12 egg yolks with 1½ cups of the sugar in the bowl, using either a whisk or an electric mixer until light and lemon colored. Add the lemon juice. (Note: It's easier to grate the zest off the lemon before squeezing the juice, so do it in that order and set the zest aside.)

When the water in the skillet is boiling, set the bowl in it and continue to beat until the egg mixture becomes smooth, creamy, and custardy. Be very careful, because if you aren't paying attention at this point, the mixture can scramble in a minute.

Scrape the mixture into a larger bowl and stir in the grated zest. Let cool, then refrigerate and chill thoroughly.

Prepare the soufflé dish. Tear off a length of waxed paper that will fit around the dish

and overlap itself by about 2 inches. Fold the paper lengthwise into thirds to make a long, thin strip, then wrap it around the upper rim of the soufflé dish to form a high collar rising above the rim. Make sure the ends overlap by at least 1 inch. Secure with string tied under the rim of the dish.

Beat the heavy cream until it starts to thicken, then add 2 teaspoons of the remaining sugar and continue to beat until the cream is stiff. Fold carefully into the chilled egg mixture.

In another, clean, dry bowl, beat the egg whites. When they start to mound, beat in the remaining ¼ cup of sugar. Keep beating until the whites hold stiff peaks, then fold them carefully into the soufflé base.

Pour into the prepared dish, smooth the top, which should come up almost to the top of the paper collar, then place the dish in the freezer for several hours or overnight, until frozen. Before serving, remove the collar and decorate the top with thin circles of sliced lemon and mint. I put a little sprig of mint right in the middle so it looks like it was growing there.

If the soufflé has been frozen overnight, you might want to leave it in the refrigerator for half an hour or so before serving so the texture won't be icy.

Crème Caramel

Serves 4 to 6

This can be made in individual cups if it is going to go on a tray, or in any 6-cup heat- and ovenproof mold or bowl. But it looks so pretty in a Charlotte mold, I always use one.

½ cup plus 3 Tablespoons sugar, divided
2 cups milk
½ vanilla bean or 1 teaspoon vanilla extract
2 eggs
4 egg yolks

Preheat the oven to 350°.

Make the caramel in a 6-cup metal Charlotte mold. Melt 3 tablespoons sugar with 1 tablespoon water. When the sugar has melted, rotate the mold to line it with the caramel. The caramel can be made in a saucepan, then poured into the mold, but it saves a step to do it the other way. Set the prepared mold aside.

Scald the milk, then stir in the remaining ½ cup sugar until it has dissolved. Add the vanilla bean and leave to infuse for 20 or so minutes. Maybe you could use the time to line the mold.

Beat the eggs and yolks together in a medium mixing bowl. Strain the milk through a fine sieve into the eggs. Stir, then skim off the froth that will have formed on the surface.

Pour the mixture into the prepared mold, then place the mold in a baking pan. Pour boiling water into the pan to come halfway up the sides of the mold. Place in the preheated oven and immediately turn the heat down to 325°. Bake for 40 minutes or until the point of a small knife poked into the center comes out clean.

Let cool completely before unmolding, using the same techniques as for the Tarte Tatin.

Strawberry Mousse

Serves 6

Before you start this, chill a pretty dish that can hold 6 cups.

1 or 2 boxes strawberries to yield 1½ cups crushed
1 cup sugar
1 teaspoon lemon juice
3 cups heavy cream
1 Tablespoon vanilla extract

Rinse and crush strawberries until you have 1½ cups of pulp. Stir in the sugar and lemon juice. Strain off any excess juice.

Beat the cream until stiff, then fold into the pulp. Stir in the vanilla.

Remove the chilled dish from the refrigerator and rinse it in cold water. Pour the strawberry mixture into the dish, cover it with plastic wrap, and freeze for 3 hours. If it has to stay frozen longer than that, place it in the refrigerator for half an hour or so before serving.

What you want is a mousse that is frozen but not icy solid. The freezing is to make the mousse firm. Some recipes use gelatin, but Madam didn't like the texture of gelatin, so I had to figure out a way to work around that.

Glorious Strawberry Mousse

Serves 8

This is another strawberry mousse, which Madam loved in spite of the tiny bit of gelatin. I don't think she really ever knew it was in this dish—another one taught me by Jean Claude Nedelec.

3 cups very ripe strawberries
¾ cup superfine sugar
1 Tablespoon unflavored gelatin
2 Tablespoons Framboise (a raspberry-flavored liqueur)
3 cups heavy cream

Wash strawberries, then remove stems and cut each strawberry into quarters. Sprinkle with sugar, toss, and refrigerate for at least half an hour.

Puree the strawberries in a food processor or through a food mill with a coarse-chopping blade. Strain through a fine sieve to remove seeds, and set aside.

In a small saucepan combine ¼ cup of the strawberry puree, the gelatin, and the *Framboise*. Heat slowly, stirring constantly until gelatin has completely dissolved.

Remove from heat and use a wire whisk to incorporate the mixture into the rest of the strawberry puree.

Whip the cream until it holds soft peaks, then stir a quarter of the whipped cream into the strawberry mixture. When it has been incorporated, use a rubber spatula to fold in the rest.

Spoon the mousse into 8 goblets and refrigerate for at least 4 hours or overnight. Decorate with fresh strawberries or raspberries and additional whipped cream if you wish.

Lace Cookies

Makes 24 cookies

Madam loved these because she always liked crunch in her food. I made them so they were almost transparent. If your first try comes out a little thicker, don't worry. With practice, you will get the confidence and the knack to make them thin.

1½ cups uncooked quick oatmeal
1½ packed cups light brown sugar
2 Tablespoons flour
½ teaspoon salt
8 Tablespoons (1 stick) butter, melted
1 egg, slightly beaten
½ teaspoon vanilla extract

Preheat the oven to 350°. Line 2 cookie sheets with aluminum foil. You can make the cookies directly on ungreased sheets, but it is easier to remove them if they are on foil and you can peel it away. And it makes the backs of the cookies shiny and pretty.

Mix together the oatmeal, brown sugar, flour, and salt in a bowl. Stir in the melted butter, the beaten egg, and then the vanilla. Make sure they are well combined and there are no lumps of brown sugar.

Drop the batter by teaspoonfuls 3 inches apart on either the foil-covered or the ungreased cookie sheets.

Bake until slightly browned, about 8–10 minutes. Let the cookies cool a bit on the baking sheets, then slide them off with a spatula as soon as they begin to get firm and let cool on racks.

These have to be watched carefully. The cookies should be very crisp but if they are underdone or too hot when you try to remove them, they will be difficult to get off the sheets or foil, and if they are overdone or have gotten too cool, they might crack. Experiment with one sheet when the cookies are still a little pale. It can always go back into the oven.

This picture of me on the beach on Skorpios shows the Christina *in the background, but it doesn't give any sense of how enormous the boat really was.*

3
MARCH

Easter Dinner in Greece

The *Christina* was just fantastic. It was like a floating hotel. There were fifty-two or so sailors and maybe five or six officers: the captain, a first officer, a radio officer, and some others. But you also had the carpenter and his crew and a whole section downstairs in the boat to do all the dry cleaning and the laundry. There were all those sailors and somebody had to do the laundry for them.

Everything was done on the boat. All the meat and fish and other supplies were shipped in from France before she sailed. Maybe they bought a very few little things when we stopped. But mostly when we were in a port, we'd go out and not come back to the boat except to sleep and have breakfast. When we were in Capri, for instance, we didn't come back for lunch. Sometimes maybe we'd return for dinner because the children got tired after a whole day. Madam and Mr. Onassis usually would be going out.

When we first started going to Skorpios, the houses weren't ready, so we lived on the boat. Then, later, it was anchored there with the sailors staying on it. After the houses were built, we mostly stayed in them, but we'd go to the boat every day. When we were living on the boat at Skorpios, Clement the chef was there with us. Later, when we were living and eating up at the houses, he would come up to cook. Then he moved into the house behind. I wasn't doing any cooking of my own yet, but I was watching Clement.

That house where he stayed was completely secluded, all the way behind the others, so it couldn't be seen. The chief mechanic and the other people who stayed on the island lived there. There was a generator near that house and all kinds of machines and a garage for the cars, but you never saw that either because that also was completely hidden. Sometimes I'd go there just to visit the people and say hi. Most of them were working on maintaining the island. They were there just to keep the island clean. They were very unsophisticated but also very nice, very lovely people. I liked to visit, and they were all happy when they saw me coming. They took out their best foods and their best drinks and were so hospitable. They were happy to see somebody, because those people were hiding constantly as they were grooming the island and watering the plants.

The house was built for them and the people from the boat. The captain always liked to stay on board in his quarters. And the first officers liked to sleep on the boat too. They would never go and live in the house. But the others didn't like to sleep on the boat because of the small cabins. When they had the chance, Clement and the others all lived off. The house had a lot of rooms, maybe fifteen or twenty. Sometimes in the summer the families of people who worked there, like Clement's wife and his children, would spend a month on Skorpios. So the help and everybody else were living in the house but you really didn't see them. They might go on the boat to eat with their husbands, but mostly they went to different beaches and they slept and lived in that house.

They had their cook there also. The Greek chef was named Master Bobby, and George was his assistant. George and Master Bobby cooked for the crew on the boat because the Greek sailors were eating Greek food, and we ate food that was more French. If we wanted to eat Greek food sometimes, we could get it from Master Bobby's kitchen or go there and taste. He was always very nice to us. Greek people are very friendly anyway. They are a little bit like Italians. They like people around and are happy to see you.

In the summers we were on Skorpios for about a month and a half, and sometimes we'd go on cruises. One time we went to all the Greek islands at once. We went to Santorini and to Olympia, Ithaca, Corfu. They're all near so you cruise a few hours and you are there. Then we would spend part of the day, usually on the island, but from these little islands we always came back to the boat for lunch and to eat dinner.

Even though there were two big dining rooms on the boat for fancy dinners, we almost always ate on the deck. Sometimes the children and I would eat in the officers' mess, not with them but after they had eaten. Mr. and Mrs. Onassis ate dinner so late, ten or eleven o'clock, that usually we couldn't wait.

The children on the trampoline on Skorpios, with Tina Radziwill looking on.

Pretty much we stayed put. But sometimes you want to have something else to do, so we didn't stay on the island all the time. Something to change the routine. I went twice to Yanina with the children. It is an old Turkish island where they have some kind of Turkish museum. It also has a fort with the guns and they still have the iron cannonballs. And some grottoes.

That is a journey. It's for the day. But we always had the captain with us or the first officer, and the Secret Service was following. They would meet us over there. Mr. and Mrs. Onassis stayed on Skorpios. They had already seen the island many times.

We saw the old fort and the terrible grottoes. Underneath. They were natural, not like the catacombs in Palermo. What a nightmare. I never will forget when we went under there. We went down and down and down, down, down. And then we walked. You walk a good twenty minutes or half an hour to reach the middle of the grotto. And then you have to walk out.

When I got to the middle, I really wanted to get out. I wanted to get out right away and I couldn't because it takes half an hour. I went in very happily ever after, and got in the middle of the grotto. Then I didn't want to be there anymore. I never thought about it until I got there. Just suddenly I felt terrible, but I didn't tell anybody. I knew I had to wait.

Later we visited Palermo and went to the catacombs there. I had never known they existed. Now I know. They are very interesting, but I didn't need to see that. Once was even

It's very faint, but you can see the smoke erupting from Mount Etna in this picture I took from the pantry.

There was always lots of the best food on the Christina, *so when this picture of John and me fishing from the deck was taken, we were just having fun. I don't remember that we ever caught anything, but if we did, Clement would have had to make a gourmet triumph of it.*

too much. That was another bad experience of my life. I had nightmares for a week. I couldn't sleep. All those threads and skeletons.

The boat stayed mainly in Europe, but the first year I came Mr. Onassis brought it to the States, and that year is when we went off cruising for a few weekends to places like Puerto Rico and around all the Virgin Islands, which was great. We went to Haiti too, which upset me very much because of the terrible poverty. On all those islands we just spent the day.

The boat was in Palm Beach, and over the Easter vacation we took a nice cruise from Palm Beach to Cozumel in Mexico. Then we came back to Palm Beach and flew back to New York.

The other years the boat sat at Skorpios. When Mr. Onassis bought Skorpios, he brought the boat to Greece and left it there. Before Mr. Onassis had Skorpios, the *Christina* was in Monte Carlo—Villefranche-sur-Mer, actually. And the boat kept going to France. I remember one year we flew from New York to Nice, boarded in Monte Carlo, and cruised all down Italy and off to Greece. The trip took ten days or maybe two weeks. It was lovely because we'd stop and swim and visit for the whole day, then cruise at night. You'd wake up in the morning in a different place.

Then I had an experience that was the opposite of the terrible times underground. One morning after we had stayed in Sardinia a few days, I went to get up and we were cruising on our way back to Greece. It's not that far to go, and we were in Greece probably that afternoon. I went to the kitchen. I was in the pantry when Charles, the butler, said, "Look,

look." There was Mount Etna, the volcano, steaming. We were cruising by. I took pictures of it. I am so lucky that I saw it. If I slept an extra hour, I would have missed it.

As I have said, I was always in the kitchen on the boat. This was long before I even had any idea that I was going to cook. But Clement was very good to me, teaching me some of his cooking tricks, which helped me afterward. These recipes are from later, because I wasn't cooking at the time we were cruising. I didn't even think about it, but I always like to learn.

Easter is an important holiday in Greece, and we would have the traditional Easter meal of roast baby lamb. That was cooked the same way a leg is: roasted with rosemary and garlic. In this country it is less usual to cook a whole lamb, so I roasted a rack of lamb, which everyone liked very much.

Mushroom Soup

Serves 8

4 ounces dried porcini mushrooms
2 cups chopped leeks (white part only)
6 Tablespoons (3/4 stick) butter
2 pounds fresh mushrooms
1/2 cup chopped fresh dill
1 clove garlic, pressed
1/4 cup chopped parsley
1 bay leaf
Salt and pepper
5 cups chicken stock (see page 132)
1 cup heavy cream

(continued on next page)

Soak the dried mushrooms for 1 hour in just enough warm water to cover them.

Wash the leeks well. Dry them and sauté them in the butter in a heavy-bottomed pot until they are wilted.

Drain the porcini mushrooms through a very fine sieve over a small bowl. Reserve the liquid. Rinse the mushrooms well and chop them fine. Wipe the fresh mushrooms clean with a damp cloth, then chop them coarsely. Add both mushrooms to the pot with the leeks and sauté them all together.

When the mushrooms begin to sweat, add the seasonings. Cook, stirring, for another minute, then add the stock and the liquid from the mushrooms. Simmer for 30 minutes.

Remove and discard the bay leaf. Let the soup cool, then puree a bit in the food processor. The finished soup should not be too smooth but have coarse bits of mushroom.

Return the soup to the pot and add the cream. Reheat carefully. This can't come to a boil, or the cream will curdle.

For this soup to be right, it must have the dried porcini, but the fresh mushrooms can be any kind. In the season I like to use whatever other wild mushrooms are available, although this will still taste great with plain white domestic mushrooms.

Roast Rack of Lamb

Serves 12

1½ cups fine dry bread crumbs
¾ cup chopped parsley
1 clove garlic, finely minced
1 Tablespoon chopped fresh rosemary
¼ cup olive oil, divided
2 double racks of lamb, trimmed
Kosher salt and pepper

Preheat the oven to 450°.

In a small bowl, mix the bread crumbs with the parsley, garlic, rosemary, and all but a tablespoon of the olive oil. Use that tablespoon of oil to brush over the lamb. Then season the lamb with salt and pepper.

Place the racks meat sides up, in a roasting pan, and spread the bread crumb mixture evenly over the meaty parts.

Roast for 15 minutes at 450°, then reduce heat to 400° and roast for another 10 minutes. Remove the racks from the oven and place them under the broiler just to give the crust some extra color.

Let the meat rest for 8 to 10 minutes before carving.

You can use more garlic or parsley or rosemary as you like, but do serve this with the Potato and Truffle Tart.

Potato and Truffle Tart

Serves 8 to 10

6 large Idaho potatoes
16 Tablespoons (2 sticks) butter, clarified (see pages 152–53)
Salt and pepper
3 to 4 black truffles, thinly sliced

Preheat the oven to 500°.

Peel the potatoes and slice them very thin. As you finish each, put the slices into a bowl of very lightly salted water. This will keep them from turning brown.

Use 2 tablespoons of the butter to coat a 10-inch pie pan generously.

Drain the potatoes, pat them dry, and toss them with a little salt and pepper. Starting in the middle of the pie pan, arrange the slices in an overlapping spiral. When one layer is finished, place some of the truffle slices over it, then brush on a coat of the butter. Continue with another layer of potatoes, then truffles, then butter, until the pie pan is completely full. End with a layer of potatoes. Place a towel over the pan and then, using another pan the same size, push down firmly on the potatoes to compress everything and make it firm.

Remove the pressing pan and the towel and pour any remaining butter over the tart.

Bake for 45 minutes or until golden brown and sizzling. Remove the tart from the oven and let it rest for 5 minutes. Then press a heated serving platter face-to-face against the rim of the pan and, holding them together and watching for butter drips, invert. If the potatoes don't release immediately, run a narrow metal spatula around the inside rim of the pan.

Slice into wedges and serve.

Pear Sorbet

Makes 3 cups

2 pounds (4 to 6) very ripe Comice pears
2 Tablespoons sugar
1 vanilla bean, split lengthwise
Juice of 1 lemon

Peel and core the pears, then place them in a pot with the sugar, vanilla bean, and ½ cup of water. Cover and cook 15 to 20 minutes until soft. Drain and put into a food processor. Add the lemon juice and puree until smooth. Let cool.

When the puree is cool, scrape it into a 3-cup half-melon mold and put it in the freezer.

When the children were young, I used to freeze the sorbet in little metal chick molds for Easter dinner. The pale yellow chicks were so cute standing on mint on the serving plate.

Just before you are ready to serve, unmold the sorbet onto a serving platter with a deep rim. Slice the sorbet between the lines of the mold, then push it back together to re-form.

Spoon a little Crème Anglaise (recipe follows) over the top and serve the rest in a separate bowl. This looks pretty garnished with little sprigs of fresh mint.

Crème Anglaise

Makes about 3 cups

2 cups milk
1 vanilla bean, split lengthwise
6 egg yolks
½ cup sugar
1 Tablespoon Poire William (a pear-flavored liqueur)

Scald the milk with the vanilla bean, then set aside. In the top of a double boiler off the heat, beat the yolks and sugar with a whisk until lemon colored.

Place the pot over simmering water in the bottom of the double boiler and, stirring constantly with a wooden spoon, slowly begin pouring in the scalded milk (with the bean still in it). Continue to pour and stir until all the milk has been added and the custard has thickened enough to coat a metal spoon—about 20 minutes.

This is a little tricky, because if the yolks get too hot, they can curdle, so keep a close watch on the heat and don't stop stirring. But if the worst happens, the custard can be saved. *Immediately* remove it from the heat and begin whisking in cold heavy cream, a little at a time. If it seems beyond that help, put 2 cups of the sauce at a time in a food processor and pulse for a few seconds until the custard reincorporates.

When the custard is ready strain it into a bowl, then add the liqueur. Place the bowl over a larger bowl of ice. Stir from time to time. When the custard is cool, cover and refrigerate until you are ready to serve it.

Mango Ice Cream

Makes 3 to 4 quarts

8 cups heavy cream
1½ cups sugar
4 cups pureed fresh mango (6 to 8 mangoes; they must be very ripe)
Juice of 3 limes, strained

Scald the cream, then, off the heat, stir in the sugar until it dissolves. At that point, stir in the mango puree and the strained lime juice. Let cool, then freeze in an ice cream machine according to the manufacturer's directions. When the ice cream is ready, store it in a container in the freezer.

This should be served the same day it is made so it doesn't get too hard. I used to scoop it out into the serving bowl a little ahead of time and leave it in the refrigerator so it would be gooey but firm. Madam always liked her ice cream slurpy.

Madam loved this ice cream, especially when I served it with a sort of julienne of fresh mango over the top. We were lucky. Jasper Johns, a friend of Madam, used to send mangoes to us from his house on Captiva.

Another good idea is to grate some fresh ginger over the ice cream just before serving. I can just see the expression on her face as she took a bite.

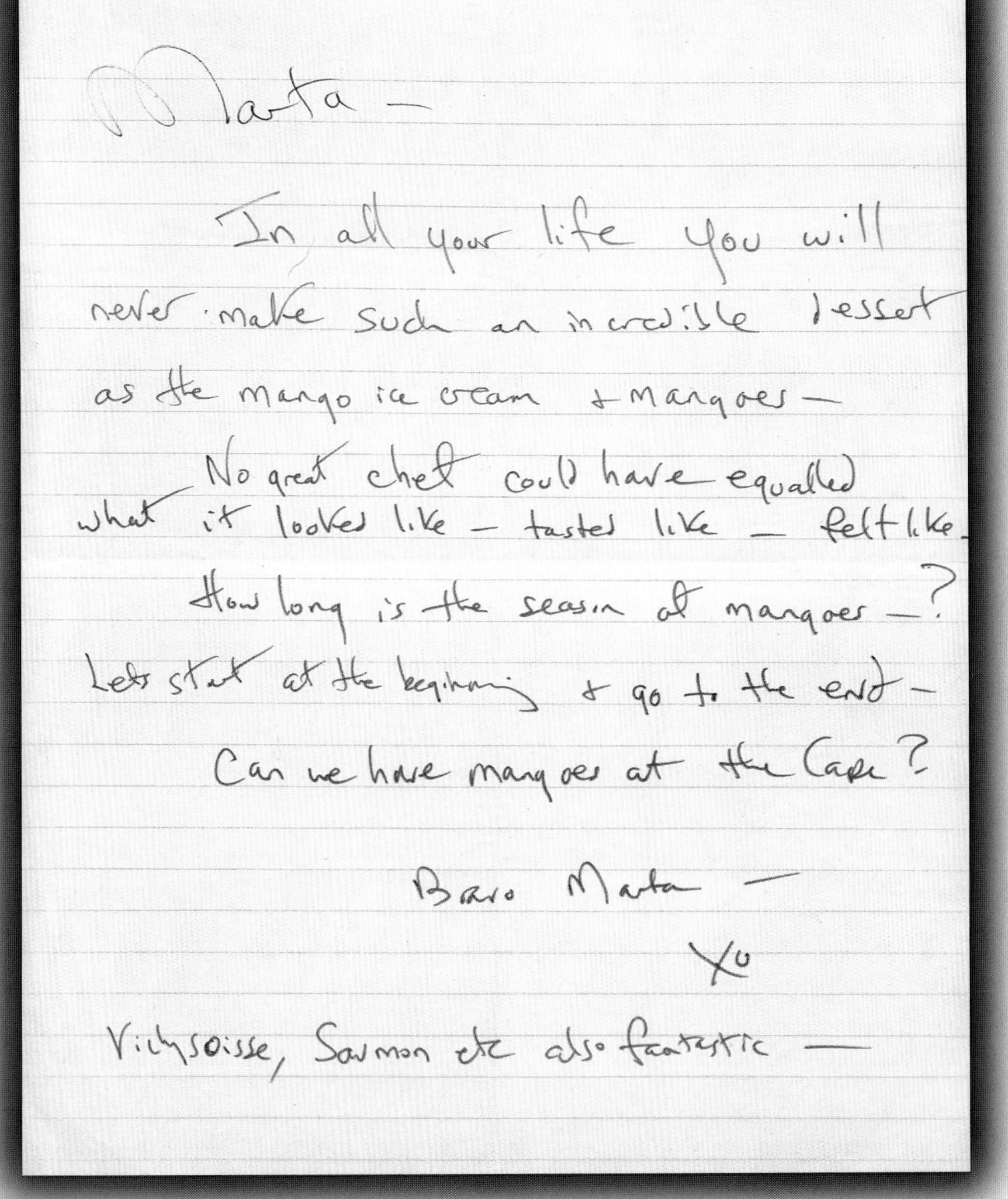
Marta —

In all your life you will
never make such an incredible dessert
as the mango ice cream + mangoes —
No great chef could have equalled
what it looked like — tasted like — felt like.
How long is the season of mangoes —?
Lets start at the beginning + go to the end —
Can we have mangoes at the Cape?

Bravo Marta —

XO

Vichysoisse, Salmon etc also fantastic —

The men with me as I survey the buffet before the guests arrive are waiters we used to hire for big parties like this one.

4

APRIL

A Dinner before the Ballet

A dinner before the ballet, usually for four people going together, was very simple and quick. It had to be fast, because the ballet was at eight o'clock, so they had to leave the house at seven-thirty. That meant we usually had dinner about six-thirty. After the theater, at ten, ten-thirty, is too late.

For centerpieces during the spring, we sometimes had tiny little lady apples. We shined them very well. And then we made a conelike pyramid in a bowl. You need a lot of them to make a nice centerpiece. And they were also to eat. Everybody picked one. Soon you need some fresh apples anyway because they wrinkle. But they stay okay for a week or so. You don't have to change the centerpiece until the next dinner. Or I used plums if I found nice ones.

When we were entertaining, we almost always had fruit, sometimes with flowers, on the tables. I did make a centerpiece with all peonies when they were in season. I cut the stems short and pushed them into a goblet or something so they were tight together and made a sort of ball. Beautiful.

The ballet season was in the spring, so we had spring food. Madam liked softshell crabs with red new potatoes—steamed with lots of parsley and butter. As a first course we would have steamed asparagus with mousseline sauce or vinaigrette. And usually I served sautéed cherry tomatoes with a little garlic. Of course, if it was a pretheater dinner I wouldn't put in garlic, just salt and pepper and lots of parsley. They tasted very good with the crabs and the little new potatoes. Dessert was always fruit dessert or fresh fruit. Light things.

Mousseline Sauce

Makes 1½ cups

16 Tablespoons (2 sticks) cold butter, divided
3 egg yolks
1 Tablespoon cold water
1 Tablespoon lemon juice
Pinch of salt
White pepper
Juice of ½ lemon
½ cup heavy cream

Melt 13 tablespoons (1½ sticks plus 1 tablespoon) of butter. Set melted butter aside.

Beat the yolks in a medium-sized saucepan for about 1 minute until they become sticky. Beat in the water, lemon juice, and salt. This will take about another half minute. Add one more last tablespoon of butter, but don't beat it in.

Place the pan over very low heat and stir with a whisk until the yolks thicken and the sauce becomes creamy. This will take a minute or two. Keep stirring. The sauce must not get lumpy. It is ready when the sauce coats the wires of the whisk.

Immediately take the pan off the heat and stir in the remaining 2 tablespoons of cold butter to stop the cooking. Then, drop by drop, begin beating in the melted butter. Keep beating the yolks and adding more butter as each addition is absorbed. When the sauce begins to thicken, the butter can be added a little faster, but keep beating. Don't add the cloudy residue at the bottom of the butter pan.

Season to taste with white pepper and lemon juice.

This is a traditional Hollandaise sauce. To make it a mousseline, beat the cream until it forms very soft peaks and fold it into the sauce just before serving.

Softshell Crabs

Serves 4

For 4 people I would buy 12 crabs because sometimes people ate 3. Softshell crabs come in small, medium, and large, and I tried to get medium. If medium wasn't available, I'd get small, never large because they were really too big.

All I did was rinse the crabs—the fish man had already cleaned them—then pat them dry and put a little lemon juice and salt and pepper on them. Then I sprinkled them with just a tiny bit of flour. If you put too much, it gets gooey, and Madam didn't like anything cooked gooey, so I just put on enough so they would get brown and crisp. Then I cooked 8 of them quickly in clarified butter. I used that because I wanted fairly high heat and I didn't want the butter to burn.

When both sides were brown and crisp, I arranged the crabs, overlapping, up one half of a long platter. If there was room, I'd put sautéed cherry tomatoes up the other side because the colors looked so pretty.

Then I deglazed the pan with some lemon juice and added some chopped parsley, and that made a sauce I poured over the crabs on the platter.

The tomatoes I just sautéed in some butter with garlic and salt and pepper. The heat

(continued on next page)

should be high, and it only takes a very little while. You just want to get them hot. I usually let one or two pop so they made a sort of sauce, but not more than that.

Steamed potatoes were served separately in their own bowl.

Before the platter went around again, I cooked the remaining crabs so that it went back with 8 crabs on it no matter how many had been taken the first time. If there was food left over, everyone was always happy to eat it up later.

Cantaloupe Sorbet

Serves 4

This is a very pure sorbet. Cantaloupe doesn't need anything done to it or added to it. Just scoop the seeds from 1 large ripe cantaloupe or 2 smaller ones, cut the rind off, and puree the flesh. Freeze in an ice cream machine according to the manufacturer's directions.

Madam loved this and I used to make it often. Usually I decorated it with little sprigs of mint, but once, because I knew it would make her happy, I decided to caramelize some strips of cantaloupe to garnish the top. It was horrible.

In Europe candied fruit is very popular. It was wonderful to bite through the sugar around an orange section or a slice of apple and get the squirt of fruit. That's what gave me the idea, but a cantaloupe is different. First of all, it is very wet, full of liquid. And then it is also slippery.

I made the sugar syrup with very little water and cut pieces of cantaloupe into little strips and dried them very well with paper towels. But when I dipped a piece into the syrup, its heat made the fruit give off more juice, and then the caramel slipped off. And if the caramel was cool enough so it didn't make the cantaloupe sweat, it was too thick and hard to stick. I spent hours dipping over and over because I had started and I am very stubborn and was determined to get it. I finally made enough for garnish, and Madam was thrilled. But even that didn't make it worth it. I never made it again.

Another dessert I made often was Cut-Up Mango with Gingerroot, which I grated and put over the mango with fresh mint.

Peel the mangos, cut out the pits, and slice them into fingers, long slices thicker than a julienne. Put the slices in a decorative bowl and grate ginger over the top, and then sprinkle on some mint leaves—whole leaves, not chopped. Then put a nice sprig in the middle. It looks like a flower.

This dessert is very good, very refreshing. Also, the mint cleans your palate. When you go to the theater, you want to have a fresh mouth. Mrs. Onassis could brush her teeth, but the guests couldn't, so that was perfect.

I prepared the mangos when the guests were eating the first course so they were sitting maybe ten minutes. They couldn't be prepared before that because the ginger will get black. Fresh ginger is okay when it's grated, but leave it a little while and it becomes black and ugly on the mangos. And sprinkle the mint just before serving. Otherwise it wilts.

Sometimes, maybe before a benefit, we would have a crowd of people to dinner before the ballet. I didn't cook for those dinners; I always used Glorious Food to cater, but I was directing the whole thing. Maybe I'd make one dish. I cooked for eight or ten people, but after that it becomes too much. Madam didn't mind. I could cook whenever I wanted or I could always get somebody in. I usually did cook. It kept me busy. We would serve those big dinners buffet style, with everything out on the table. Everyone would take a plate and the waiters would serve them, then all that would be cleared away and dessert, usually fruit, and coffee would be put out.

A typical buffet table would have a Poached Salmon with Green Sauce, Jambon Persillée, a cucumber salad, a Russian salad of grated celeriac or some other root vegetable, slices of pâté, which I bought, and a basket or platter of good, chewy bread, which I also bought. I would often set out hulled strawberries on the table too because they looked so pretty.

To make JAMBON PERSILLÉE, buy a good big ham, the kind you would serve for Easter. Nowadays you can buy hams cooked. While you are at the butcher, also get some veal bones to make BASIC STOCK. You make it with one large peeled onion, five celery stalks, four scraped carrots, a small bunch of parsley, salt and peppercorns all boiled up in six quarts of cold water with about three pounds of the good bones and about three pounds of chicken backs and necks. The bones will give the stock a little thickening, and the rest will flavor it.

First you slice all the ham off the bone, then you chop the slices into little pieces. What you want is little bits of ham.

Then you need a mold, or you can use a large round bowl. Press the little pieces of ham into the bowl so the meat becomes a tight mass, weight it down, and leave for about half an hour.

Meanwhile, dissolve gelatin in the stock. The thickening from the bones won't be enough to make an aspic. Pour the stock over the ham pressed in the mold and let it penetrate all the way down. Keep pouring until you see liquid again at the top. Then cover and refrigerate overnight. This gives the juices time to incorporate.

When you are ready to serve, chop a lot of parsley *very* fine. If it is fine enough, it will get wet. Turn the mold over on a decorative platter and remove the mold. Then press the parsley all over the surface of the ham mold.

Slice at the table.

Marta

Dick Goodwin will be coming for supp
tomorrow night - Wednesday - But I dont want
you to cook it - I want you to come to
Gallaghers with us -

So why dont you make a casserole
Coq au Vin or Navarin or Boeuf Bourguignon.
Francisco can give us that & a salad -
For dessert - have him get one of those paper
thin apple tartes from Zabars - He can warm
it & serve with vanilla ice cream -

Whole Poached Salmon

Serves 8

1 cup dry white wine
2 bay leaves
3 sprigs parsley
1 stalk celery
3 sprigs fresh dill
2 branches fresh thyme
1 small onion, peeled and quartered
10 black peppercorns
1 teaspoon salt
1 (5-pound) salmon, cleaned and dressed

Add all the ingredients but the salmon to 2 quarts of water, and bring to a boil. Boil, uncovered, for 25 minutes, then strain the court bouillon through a double thickness of cheesecloth into a large bowl. Discard the flavorings.

Wrap the salmon in cheesecloth to help it hold together, then place it in a fish poacher or some other long, covered oval kettle that will hold the fish. If you use a kettle, place a rack on the bottom. Arrange the fish so that the loose ends of the cheesecloth are on top. Pour in the strained court bouillon, cover, and bring the liquid to a simmer. Simmer for 40 minutes. It is important that the liquid never boils; it might disintegrate the fish.

Lift the rack with the fish out of the poacher or kettle. Remove the cheesecloth and peel the skin from the fish. Very carefully scrape away any dark flesh.

Cool to room temperature, then chill for 8 to 10 hours.

This can now be served as is with Green Sauce or, for a fancier presentation, arrange the fish on a serving platter and glaze with aspic (this is the court bouillon with gelatin dis-

(continued on page 82)

solved in it). Paint a layer of the warm, partially gelled aspic onto the fish. As it dries, paint on another, over and over.

When the aspic was partly set, I would decorate the top of the fish. I made a flower with a black truffle for the blossom and tarragon leaves for the greens. Then I decorated the platter by arranging around the edge lemon halves wrapped in muslin so they didn't squirt when they were squeezed. Among them I put little cherry tomatoes and deviled egg halves. I took the yolks out of hard-boiled eggs, mashed them with a little mayonnaise and dry mustard, and then stuffed this mixture back into the whites.

This, too, can be served with Green Sauce (recipe follows).

Green Sauce

For this sauce to work, all the ingredients have to be at room temperature.

MAYONNAISE

3 egg yolks

1 Tablespoon lemon juice or wine vinegar

Salt and white pepper

Powdered mustard

2¼ cups olive oil or canola if you prefer

GREENS

¼ cup minced fresh spinach

¼ cup minced watercress leaves

¼ cup minced parsley

2 Tablespoons minced fresh chives

1 teaspoon minced fresh tarragon

In a warm, medium-sized bowl beat the yolks with a wire whisk for a minute or two until they are sticky. Stir in the vinegar and salt, pepper, and mustard to your taste, then beat just to incorporate, less than a minute.

Now start adding the oil. A warning: You can't stop beating once you begin this process.

Begin dripping it in, a drop at time, beating constantly. As the yolks absorb the oil, add a little more, and then a little more until about half a cup of oil has been incorporated and the mixture is the consistency of a medium gravy. Then you can begin adding more oil, a tablespoon or two at a time.

Keep adding and beating until the sauce is the consistency you want. If it gets too thick, you can add more vinegar or lemon juice. To thicken, keep adding oil. You may not want to add the whole amount called for. It will yield about 2½ cups.

Blanch the spinach, watercress, a little parsley for the color, the chives, and the tarragon in ¼ cup water, covered, in a small pan. Simmer about 3 minutes, then press into a fine sieve briefly to drain.

Stir the minced greens into the mayonnaise. That's all there is to it. Serve with the poached salmon.

At this point I have to tell the story about Chester. He was my pigeon. I say *my* pigeon, but really he was just a regular New York pigeon who started to come to the kitchen window. I would leave the window open and feed him on the sill. I know pigeons are dirty and carry disease, but poor animal, I had trained him to come.

One day I had poached a salmon and it was out cooling so I could take the skin off. I had gone back to my room for something, and suddenly Efigénio, the butler, came running and said, "Marta, come quickly to the kitchen. Your son is eating the salmon." "Your son." I'll never forget it.

Of course, I had to do another whole salmon, because even though Chester hadn't really messed it at all, I couldn't take the chance and serve that one.

I didn't have to look good to go into the garden. If I did this picture would have made the tomatoes red.

5
May

Children's Cookouts

Every year, Madam and I only came to the house on Martha's Vineyard for weekends for the first month, and we were usually alone. Sometimes it was even cold or raining, so you couldn't go to the beach. I always brought a lot of supplies with me and decided ahead of time what I was going to make for dinner that night. We'd fly up and get there around two o'clock, so if I wanted fish, I'd go to the fish market in Menemsha, which is very near. But if I wanted meat, I brought it because I didn't want to go all the way to Vineyard Haven to get it. If I knew I wanted to do something special, I'd bring the ingredients. Nothing much was growing yet. But the vegetables were already started in the garden: peas and little baby carrots and salad. That was enough.

Sometimes when it was just the two of us, I'd make Madam a surprise dinner, and she was always so happy and grateful. She especially liked grilled Dover sole with Chive Sauce and lemon wedges. Or I'd have a VEAL CHOP WITHOUT THE BONE. I'd get one about an inch and a half thick and cut a pocket in it. Then I'd fill the pocket with vegetable mirepoix (finely chopped aromatic vegetables sautéed in butter) and use a toothpick to keep it closed while I sautéed it quickly in butter. I kept it hot on a plate as I deglazed the pan with port or marsala. Then I poured the sauce over the chop on the plate and also served Chive Sauce with that. And when Madam was alone, she didn't want a starch, so I'd make two vegetables. Maybe it would be julienned vegetables or cabbage and carrots sautéed in sesame oil or steamed broccoli or cauliflower.

Madam liked all kinds of vegetables, so we always had several. She would like them one way and then I made them a different way if children were eating with us. You can't give children too strong vegetables. They're too soon for that.

An example was Madam would have her spinach stewed or as soup, but for small children I served it creamed. Madam also liked kale and Swiss chard, which I made by removing the stems and then sautéing. She liked kohlrabi, and in the spring I would make dandelion greens. I steamed and sautéed them with garlic if Madam wasn't going out after.

She also loved braised vegetables, and in the winter we would have braised endive or fennel at least once a week. We also had braised Boston lettuce.

When I made beets, which Madam also liked very much, I would bake or boil or steam them. In the summer I picked them when they were the size of marbles and served them with their little stems on. If they were bigger, I took off the stems and ate the greens myself.

Because Madam didn't like to fuss with her food, when I served artichokes, it was usually trimmed so she had just the hearts. I would then stew the hearts, cut in two, in a very tiny amount of water until they were cooked. If I could find the babies, where you can eat everything, I first trimmed them a little, then I steamed them in the pot in olive oil with salt and pepper and garlic and parsley for about 45 minutes. They were great.

Madam's great favorite was EGGPLANT FRITTERS. She said she could eat them every day if they weren't so fattening. But sometimes I'd make them as a special treat for her, or she would have a big basket of them on the table for an informal dinner.

To make them, I sliced the eggplant thin, then sprinkled it with salt and put it between layers of paper towels with weights on it. That was so all the juice sweated out. When it seemed enough had come I would pat the slices dry, dip them just the littlest bit in flour, just so they would get a crust, and deep-fry them. They were like better potato chips.

I always brought fruit enough for the weekend. With just Madam and me alone, how much could we eat? I would buy only enough that it got eaten in two, three days and not

The table in the corner of the patio where guests picked up their plates and cups and utensils. The food was laid out on the big dining table.

spoil out of the refrigerator. I left fruit out because when fruit is cold, it tastes different. Apples are fine, and oranges, cherries also, grapes. But peaches and plums and nectarines and apricots, for me the refrigerator is a no-no.

The minute the children came, it all changed. They usually had friends with them, and suddenly there were lots of people all around. It is still like that on the Vineyard and Long Island. And a good way, if you are having lots of guests, is a cookout.

We had hot dogs and hamburgers, and the children helped. And I made salads. I usually made a potato salad or cucumber with dill and sour cream. I have a good secret for my POTATO SALAD. I suppose everybody has it. You cook the potatoes and then you cut them in pieces, and then, when they're still warm, that's the time you have to season them. They keep the flavor and the taste much better. I usually add chives, not onions, I think they are too strong, too sharp, and the taste comes up to you. And salt and pepper and oil and vinegar. The salad is much lighter without mayonnaise. And much tastier. Believe me, they're delicious. Everyone loves it that way, when you can taste just the potatoes. And if you season them when they are warm and you don't put them in the refrigerator, it gives a different taste altogether. Like the fruit. I don't like the changed taste when the salad has been chilled.

I discovered this because if you have leftovers and eat them the following day, they don't have the same taste. Refrigeration kills the taste of a lot of things besides fruit and potatoes. Ed Schlossberg always teases me and says, I know you don't believe in refrigerators. And I say I do believe but only for what should be refrigerated.

Once I was making something when Anthony Radziwill was there and I told him it wouldn't be ready until that night for dinner. He wanted to taste it then, and I said, You can't taste it now because it has to become a certain temperature before you eat it. So he asked me why I didn't put it in the refrigerator. My answer was, you can't brutalize my food. So now he keeps saying that to me: "You can't brutalize my food." He got such a kick out of it. But what I said is right: food has to take its time; you can't rush it.

If the cookout was for grownups as well as children, I'd have real meat, not just hot dogs and hamburgers. I'd marinate the meat. Sometimes I'd cook a BUTTERFLIED LEG OF LAMB that I marinated in garlic and mustard. Not too much olive oil, because when you barbecue, the oil drips and burns. So you have to use very little. And rosemary, of course, and salt and pepper. I usually marinate things for a long time. If I start marinating too early, I do put the meat in the refrigerator, but then I take it out an hour before cooking. I want it to be at room temperature. You can't cook it when it is too cold. It shivers. It is like us. Even if the meat is dead, it doesn't matter.

And there would always be a big green salad with different greens, maybe red leaf and butter crunch lettuce, some arugula, and chopped chives, oregano, and basil with a vinaigrette.

For dessert we had peach pies. I make an excellent Deep-Dish Peach Pie. We always had cookies and often my Summer Pudding or a tart on the table. And I usually had a nice watermelon. It's summery, you know. And then I'd have maybe a fruit salad.

We had another kind of cookout for special occasions. On Labor Day there was a party on the beach for about 120 people—too many—so it was catered. Usually we had a clam chowder, all kinds of chicken, hamburgers, hot dogs, all that stuff. And mozzarella and tomatoes from the garden. That one I served at the smaller cookouts too. Always a tray of mozzarella, tomato, and basil. Lots of basil, a good olive oil. I quartered the tomatoes and served them in a bowl. There was a deli in Vineyard Haven that sold good mozzarella. Then we had fruit salad.

Sometimes if I couldn't find the cheese or something else I needed, I would go to a restaurant and get them to sell it to me. When I needed something—you name it—I had to have it.

And for cheese my best bet was the restaurants. I was taking my chances. They didn't know who I was or where I came from or anything. But usually I was pretty successful. Nothing stopped me. Like when I'm buying my vegetables, I never go to the store; I go to the farms and I choose each tomato separately. I'm always determined to get the best, the freshest.

For instance, in 1991 Hurricane Bob destroyed everything on the island. A week after the hurricane, at the end of August, it was Mr. Templesman's birthday and I was determined to have a sunflower. We had a tradition that whoever had a birthday in the summer always had a sunflower on his chair. We grew them around the house. But that year there was no such a thing. You couldn't find a sunflower on the island. I finally discovered that behind the Mid-Island garage there was a farm where a man had been raising sunflowers. So I said to myself, the hurricane was here, I understand, but it might have left one or two in his field; he had so many. And one week after the storm there may be ones that were sprouting, and didn't have a chance to open. With phone calls, I finally found the name of the man. He said okay, get as many as you want. And in between all the destroyed sunflowers in the field, I could get enough for a nice bouquet. I was all bruised, all scratched, but I got the whole back of the car full of sunflowers. And he didn't even charge me very much. Madam said, "I can't believe it: sunflowers on Martha's Vineyard after a hurricane."

Madam's blue-and-white table ready, with the ceremonial sunflower, for Mr. Templesman's birthday.

I mostly made all the salads the same way: the main food—the potatoes or the mussels or whatever—in a vinaigrette made with red wine or balsamic vinegar, different herbs, and olive oil. No one in the family likes mayonnaise much. The big difference was in the herbs I used, only one for each salad. You can use more, but then you taste only the herbs. I mostly stayed out of the garlic because if it wasn't cooked it bothered Madam.

A vinaigrette sauce is just a mixture of oil and vinegar seasoned with salt and pepper.

Sometimes I used lemon juice instead of vinegar and sometimes chopped herbs such as chives, thyme, basil, or tarragon. And sometimes I added mustard. Everybody has his or her own idea of what the proportions should be. That's up to your personal taste. It depends on what the vinaigrette is being served with.

I almost never taste as I'm cooking. Most people who cook all the time don't. The exception is when I'm making a vinaigrette. I always keep tasting then, because I think that's the only way I can really know if it's right.

Simple Mustard Vinaigrette

Makes enough for 2 to 3 bowls of salad

1 teaspoon dry mustard
1½ teaspoons Dijon mustard
¼ cup balsamic vinegar
¾ cup olive oil

Stir the mustards into the vinegar until they are completely mixed, then beat in the olive oil.

For Tuna Salad I started with tuna—sometimes fresh tuna, sometimes from the can. Canned tuna which is dark inside is fine; you don't have to use white meat. Sometimes I put little red peppers in the salad. I cooked them ahead of time and then seasoned them. And when the peppers got to room temperature, I put in avocado, grated carrots, celery, and tomatoes. I just did that when somebody came for lunch who wasn't expected. By the time you eat that salad it becomes a whole meal.

Many times I made a Corn Salad. First of all, I used fresh corn. I boiled it, then took the kernels off the cob. And then I added a little bit of sweet bell pepper to give taste and some color—a little green and a little red. And the same old seasoning: salt and pepper. I didn't put any tomato or any parsley or chives in the corn, I know that. Maybe some dill. I kept the salad plain because corn is so good by itself. And I used regular vinegar, not balsamic. The balsamic gives a color sometimes, and you don't want to see the corn turning brown because of the balsamic vinegar.

Ed taught me about CABBAGE SALAD, coleslaw. He likes it very much. He shreds the cabbage and then he puts in some caraway and some celery seeds, some mustard powder, some vinegar, some mayonnaise, and quite a bit of pepper and garlic salt. It comes a little hot.

He's usually the cabbage specialist, but sometimes I make it my way too. I put nothing on it. I just take grated cabbage and then I season it. Even if I use some mayonnaise, I always dilute it with a little cream or a little milk if I have it. That makes it much thinner and tastier, not pasty like mayonnaise can be. I don't like to put too much on food. Mayonnaise takes away the taste of the lobster or the corn or whatever is the main ingredient of the salad. And then, because it's so thick, you have to stir it and stir it and then the salad looks mooshy. And sometimes fragile food like lobster breaks. If you start with about a tablespoon of mayonnaise and add a little bit of light cream and then mix in all the seasonings, you get a thick enough sauce. And you pour that on top of your food and when you toss it lightly, it coats very well and everything stays in one piece.

Madam loved my CARROT SALAD. She always would ask me what I did to make it taste so good, better than anyone else's, and I told her nothing special. She thought it tasted like nuts, but really all it was was the grated carrots, lots of chopped parsley, and the vinaigrette. It was the most simple thing. I peeled the carrots, then I'd grate them in the Cuisinart. It was easier than grating by hand and it also gave a better texture. Then it was the same old thing. Lots of chopped parsley, salt and pepper, oil and vinegar. And that was all. And you see, if you do the carrots a little bit ahead of time, again, they soak up the vinaigrette and they become very tasty.

I made the BEET SALAD with the beets boiled first, then cooled a little, and peeled and julienned, mixed with chopped chives and the vinaigrette. Again, don't let the beets cool too much or they won't soak up the flavors as well.

Senator Kennedy loves this. When he heard about this book, he said to put him down for Lobster Salad and Beet Salad. I already had, but I didn't tell him. Once we were going to have a cookout and I was making salads when Uncle Teddy arrived. When he visits, he always comes into the kitchen and tastes everything. I like that when a man comes to the kitchen and tries what I'm cooking. I had the beet salad ready in a bowl and was making something else. The senator came right away into the kitchen and went for his favorite. While we were talking, he was picking at it and nibbling. When he was ready to leave, he said he hoped there would be some beet salad left for him to take home. I looked and said I'd just put what was there in a container for him because now there wasn't enough to serve. Luckily, there was a lot of other food and the cookout was a big success.

Nowadays you can get pretty good tomatoes all year, but I always think of TOMATO SALAD as something I made on the Vineyard when they were ripe in our garden. Every morning the gardener would ask me what I wanted him to pick for me, but I always told him nothing because I liked to go myself and see what vegetables looked good to me that day and choose the ones I wanted. I wanted to have the smell and the feel myself. If Madam was alone, she liked to eat tomato salad every day for lunch when they were in season. I made my salad with peeled tomatoes cut into wedges with chopped basil and vinaigrette. Some people like to eat tomatoes with the skin on, and there's nothing wrong with that. I just think they taste better peeled, but then they have to be perfectly ripe. If the seeds were really big, sometimes I'd take out some of them. But not all, because they give flavor.

My garden had only red tomatoes, but sometimes if we went to Nantucket, I'd get some of the beautiful yellow ones and add a few for color.

I made an elegant salad for a first course, with green beans and pâté, and the recipe is here in the book on page 43. But if we were just going to have some vegetable salads, I did the GREEN BEAN SALAD more simply. I snapped them then steamed them a very little, I mixed them with finely chopped shallots, parsley, and the vinaigrette. Again, I could have used onions, but they are too strong, so I mostly put shallots into salads.

For both ZUCCHINI and CUCUMBER SALADS, the herb I used was chopped dill. The zucchini I would cut into little sticks but bigger than a julienne, maybe 3 or 4 inches long and about ¼ inch wide, and steam just for a second. Cucumbers were raw, of course. I peeled them, then cut them into very, very thin slices or little chunks. These were good as a salad on

their own but also to go with cold salmon. The vinaigrette I used with cucumber salad had a little more vinegar than usual because vinegar is such a good taste with cucumbers.

When I made a corn salad, I would use finely diced green and red peppers to add a little extra color. But if I made a PEPPER SALAD alone, I still tried to use several different colors—red, orange, and yellow if I could find them—along with the green. I would steam the peppers and put them hot into a paper bag to loosen the peel, or that can also be done by charring them. Then I seeded them and sliced them into really thick sticks, and I seasoned them only with salt and pepper, and a light vinaigrette.

I made KIDNEY BEAN SALAD too, but I always only used one color, the light ones. Other people mix them, but I liked the way they looked better if it was all one color in the bowl.

UNCLE TEDDY'S FAVORITE LOBSTER SALAD

Serves 8

When you cook lobsters, you have to get them fresh, not making them suffer, then they stay very good. We had our own pots on the Vineyard, so we could just ask in the morning and have lobsters fresh from the pond for lunch or dinner.

6 ears of corn
4 pounds lobster meat (about 8 medium lobsters)
2 large tomatoes
2 ripe avocados
1 Tablespoon mayonnaise
2 Tablespoons milk
½ cup chopped fresh dill
Salt and pepper

Cook the corn, then scrape off the kernels over a bowl. Set aside.

Boil the lobsters for 15 minutes. Remove them from the pot, drain well, and place on a work surface. Cut off the claws, crack them, and remove the meat to a large bowl. Slit the lobster tails down the underside and remove the meat. Cut all the meat, tail and claws, into bite-sized pieces and replace in the bowl.

Peel, seed, and chop the tomatoes into small pieces. Peel, pit, and cut the avocado into small cubes. Put the tomato, avocado, and corn in the bowl with the lobster and mix gently.

In a small bowl, combine the mayonnaise with the milk (or you can use light cream). Mix together well until smooth. Sprinkle dill, salt, and pepper over the lobster mixture, then add the mayonnaise and stir briefly so the sauce barely holds the rest of the ingredients together. Cover, and refrigerate for a few hours before serving.

Caroline is sure I use celery in this salad, but really, these are the ingredients—no celery.

Chive Sauce

Makes 2 cups

Madam specially liked this sauce with Dover sole, which I marinated in olive oil and salt and pepper and then grilled on top of the stove. She thought it made the fish taste almost like meat.

2 Tablespoons chopped shallots
¼ cup white wine
4 teaspoons chicken stock (see page 132)
1½ cups heavy cream
1 Tablespoon pureed watercress
3 Tablespoons cold water

(continued on next page)

1 Tablespoon finely chopped chives
6½ Tablespoons (¾ stick) butter, softened
1 Tablespoon lemon juice
Salt and pepper

In a small saucepan, bring the shallots and wine to a boil and continue to boil, uncovered, until almost all the wine has evaporated. You should end up with about 1 tablespoon of damp, softened shallots. Remove the pan from the heat and set it aside.

In a second small saucepan, combine the stock with the cream. Again, bring to a boil and boil, uncovered, until the mixture is reduced by about one-third. It should be very rich and creamy. Remove this pan from the heat and set aside.

Scrape the softened shallots into a blender, add the pureed watercress, the water, the chives, and the butter. Blend for 30 seconds. Add the reduced cream and the lemon juice. Blend again until smooth. Taste and season with salt and pepper if needed.

The sauce should be served hot. It can be kept warm in the top of a double boiler, but make sure it doesn't come to a boil again or it might curdle.

❋

This is delicious served with the broiled sole or with veal steaks. I sometimes used to sneak out and grill both of these and other meat or fish on a little hibachi on the terrace. I knew it's against the law in New York City, but the result seemed worth the risk. Madam would always say, "This is so good! How do you do it?" And my answer always was "You don't want to know."

That was often our arrangement. For instance, I got so I hated flying in little airplanes like the one that goes from Newark to Martha's Vineyard. Even though Madam kept telling me I was being paranoid, she was very sympathetic. She agreed we could take the shuttle to Boston and then the little commuter plane only the few minutes from there to the Vineyard. We had some of our most personal conversations in that Boston airport waiting for the connection.

Madam was most comfortable if she could have a seat in the first row so everyone didn't have to walk past her all the time. And she always took the window seat for the same reason. I sort of resented that, but I could understand. There are no reserved seats on the shuttle, and she used to ask me sometimes how I always managed to get us the ones she wanted. Again I would tell her, "You don't want to know."

She didn't like to ask for special favors, but her name was magic.

Summer Pudding

Serves 6 to 8

Because everyone loved my summer pudding, I made it a lot. Once Rose Styron asked Madam for the recipe, so I gave it to her and she wrote it down very carefully and then read it to Mrs. Styron. Later Mrs. Styron was complaining because her summer pudding didn't taste as good as mine, and Madam asked her if she had followed the recipe exactly. Because it was summer and we were all on the Vineyard, Mrs. Styron hadn't been able to get the little imported red currants (I would buy lots of them in New York and keep them in the freezer, or have someone who was coming bring them). So she had used some other kind of berry. Madam told her, "You see, you have to do it just like Marta says or it won't turn out."

4 cups raspberries
4 cups blueberries
1 cup red currants
¾ cup sugar
8 to 10 slices good-quality firm white sandwich bread, crusts removed

(continued on next page)

Combine the berries with the sugar in a saucepan and stew them for only 2 to 4 minutes. Don't add any water. The berries will make their own juice as they cook.

Leave the berries to cool. Meanwhile, line the bottom and sides of a round, deep, ovenproof dish—a 7-cup soufflé dish is perfect—with the bread. The dish shouldn't be deeper than about 3½ inches or the pudding will be soggy. And the bread must form a tight lining. There should be no space the juice can escape through. You can patch with little pieces of bread.

Spoon the cooled fruit over the bread, reserving about ½ cup of the juice.

Cover the top of the fruit completely with a layer of bread, again with no gaps.

Find a plate that exactly fits inside the rim of the baking dish, and place it over the top of the pudding. On top of the plate, arrange 3 pounds of weight. Cans of food or juice are convenient for this. Refrigerate overnight.

Just before serving, remove the weights and plate and invert a round rimmed platter over the pudding. Don't use a flat platter or the juice will overflow. Turn the dish and platter over together so the platter is on the bottom, then remove the dish, leaving the pudding on the platter. Pour the reserved ½ cup of juice over the top.

Serve with thick fresh cream or Crème Fraîche (recipe follows), but it is almost more delicious without.

Crème Fraîche

This is more like the French cream.

1 teaspoon buttermilk
1 cup heavy cream

In a small saucepan, stir the buttermilk into the cream, then heat to body temperature. It shouldn't feel even a bit hot. Pour into a jar and cover, but don't screw the lid on tight. Let stand at room temperature until the mixture has thickened. This will take as little as an afternoon on a hot day or as much as 3 days if it is cold. When the cream does get thick, stir, cover tightly, and refrigerate. It will keep there for a week or more.

Madam and Rose Styron chatting on the beach. Maybe they were talking about the Summer Pudding.

Deep-Dish Peach Pie

CREAM CHEESE CRUST

8 Tablespoons (1 stick) butter, softened

8 Tablespoons (4 ounces) cream cheese, softened

1½ cups flour

2 Tablespoons sugar

¼ teaspoon salt

2 Tablespoons heavy cream

Beat the butter and cream cheese together in a large bowl with a large spoon. The mixture is ready when it is smooth and fluffy.

Sift the flour, sugar, and salt together over the mixture, then pour in the cream. Use your hands to mix thoroughly until the dough can be gathered into a compact ball. Dust the dough with flour, wrap in waxed paper, and refrigerate while you prepare the filling.

FILLING

2 pounds fresh ripe peaches

1 Tablespoon flour

2 Tablespoons brown sugar

4 Tablespoons (½ stick) butter, melted

3 teaspoons vanilla

1 egg yolk lightly beaten with 2 teaspoons cold water

1 teaspoon sugar

Preheat the oven to 350° and set a rack at the middle level.

The peaches should be peeled. An easy way to do this is to bring a saucepan of water to a boil and lower the peaches into it one or two at a time. Scoop them out of the water after

30 seconds, and while they are still warm, you will be able to slip the skin off easily with the help of a sharp knife. If the skin resists at all, put the peaches back into the water for a few more seconds.

Over a large bowl, to catch any juice, cut the peaches into thin slices. Add the flour, brown sugar, melted butter, and vanilla and mix it all together gently but thoroughly. Move the mixture to an 8-inch-diameter soufflé dish or any other attractive ovenproof dish or bowl of roughly the same shape with the same 11-cup capacity. Bury 2 peach pits in the filling to add more flavor. Spread the surface to even it.

On a lightly floured surface, roll out the pastry into an 11-inch circle. Lift it up over the rolling pin and gently drape it over the top of the peaches. Trim the dough so the overhang is about an even inch. Crimp the edges neatly and paint the entire surface with the egg/water wash. Sprinkle the top of the pastry with the sugar and cut 2 small slits to allow steam to escape.

Bake for 35 to 40 minutes or until the crust is golden brown. Serve directly from the dish, and don't forget to warn guests about the hidden pits.

Brownies

These brownies originally came from Glorious Food. Everyone loved them, especially Madam, who always liked crunch in her food, so I got the recipe from Jean Claude and then, being me, changed it.

7 ounces unsweetened chocolate
16 Tablespoons (2 sticks) unsalted butter, at room temperature
1¾ cups sugar
5 large eggs, at room temperature
1 cup sifted unbleached flour
2 Tablespoons vanilla extract
¼ teaspoon salt
5 ounces good chunk bittersweet chocolate, chopped into ½-inch bits

Preheat the oven to 350°.

Lightly butter a 13 x 9 x 2-inch pan, then line it with waxed paper. Butter the paper, then dust with flour, and shake out any excess. Set aside.

In the top of a double boiler over low heat, melt the unsweetened chocolate. When it is melted, remove from heat and let cool to room temperature.

Beat the butter and the sugar together in an electric mixer at slow speed until light and thoroughly blended. Raise beater speed to medium and add the eggs one at a time, scraping sides of the bowl after each addition. Beat until fluffy.

Beat in the flour to blend thoroughly, then add the vanilla and the salt. Fold in the melted chocolate thoroughly, then fold in the bittersweet chocolate bits.

Pour the batter into the prepared pan and even the top with a rubber spatula. Bake 18 to 20 minutes or just until a toothpick stuck into the center comes out almost but not quite clean. The timing is important because this is a mousselike brownie and the center should be slightly underbaked. While the brownies are baking, line a cookie sheet with waxed paper.

Remove the brownies from the oven. Immediately cover the brownies with the lined cookie sheet, paper against the brownies, and carefully turn the 2 pans over so that the brownies drop onto the cookie sheet. Peel off the waxed paper that is now on top and refrigerate the brownies until they are cold. Cut into 1½- to 2-inch squares using a long thin-bladed knife. Clean the blade after each cut.

Store at room temperature in an airtight container or wrapped in foil. Serve at room temperature. Ideally, these should be eaten within 24 hours.

I was just starting breakfast in this picture taken in the Vineyard kitchen.

6

JUNE

Day-to-Day Summer Eating on Martha's Vineyard

At the Vineyard everybody lives on the beach, swimming and sailing and water-skiing. They are there for most of the day, and I don't see them. When John and Caroline were young, we swam all summer because we were in Greece most of the time. Nowadays on Long Island there is a pool, so even if the ocean is rough, everybody can still swim all summer.

On Martha's Vineyard at the beginning of the summer we usually were there only weekends, but then we were there full-time. This was a great vacation for all of us, but Madam was always in touch with her office in New York. There was a fax machine set up in the guest room near her bedroom, and one day when Madam was going upstairs, a fax started to come in and she was stopped by the noise. This was about the fifth one of the day, and it was only morning. She looked at the machine and muttered that it sounded like "an angry canary squeaking and squeezing out miles of toilet paper." She could be so funny.

Hyannis was great for the children because they had all their cousins there and lots of sports. Mrs. Onassis wasn't playing those team sports. What she did more was skiing—both snow and water—and riding. Especially riding. But that was more in the fall.

In summer the children were going sailing every single day and then swimming, and

Someone would look at this and think, what sort of cook is that, posing on her butcher board? Just me, kidding around.

This is the table on the patio where we ate lunch. We all loved the view over the pond.

there was a boat, a Chris-Craft, so we could water-ski. The *PT-109.* It's on the Vineyard now. There was a little Greek sailor named Vassili whose job was cleaning and taking care of the boat and taking people water-skiing. Madam was the main one going water-skiing, and the children. I guess the cousins were probably going too. But Madam water-skied every day, twice a day actually. She loved it. She was so straight on those skis; she was like a bullet.

She liked to swim and she liked to run on the beach and she loved to water-ski, but she wasn't really a sailor. But the children, especially when we were in Greece, were sailing all the time. They always had the little Sunfish boats and then sailing dinghies, and a lot of the aunts and uncles had bigger sailing boats.

All summer all the children were in the kitchen constantly. They had breakfast in the kitchen. And at breakfast kids play, so they were in the kitchen until twelve o'clock. Then it's lunchtime. But on good days they'd go to the beach and come back around two to have lunch, and then they are back out. So they let me do my things.

The kitchen was planned to have lots of people in it. Madam always said how much she wanted the kitchen to be homey. When the Vineyard house was first built, it bothered her that the kitchen was too neat and perfect. But I reassured her that very soon it would get to look lived in, which is what she preferred.

Everyone always liked to eat light vegetable and seafood salads for lunch if the weather was warm. We always had a variety of maybe four or five. And we ate whatever vegetables were ripe in the garden. There was always iced tea ready with mint from the garden to go with whatever anyone was eating. If I wasn't sure what time people would be back from the beach, salads could wait, or if Madam was having lunch with a friend, I would serve something like Vitello Tonnato with salads on trays and give them their privacy.

No matter if we were eating breakfast in the kitchen or lunch out on the terrace, cooking was my territory. If we were having a cookout, sometimes one of the men wanted to grill, and if we were doing that or having lunch outside, the kids would help me get the dishes and bring them out or back inside. But the cooking and the shopping, no.

John had this shirt made as part of my gift when Caroline and he gave me my little white car.

That was mainly why I got my driver's license. Before that, when we were going to Hyannis, someone had to drive me to the market. I would have had to drive anyway once we had the house on the Vineyard, because it is so far from anything else. But before that I knew it was time when Madam said to me one day, "You make friends with everyone everywhere you go; why don't you make friends with a taxi driver?" Then, when I did get my license, she and the children were so proud. They gave me my little white car for my birthday that year.

Mostly I knew who was eating at the house, and so I could fix the menu for the situation. In summer if we had hors d'oeuvres, they would be something cold like Oeufs en Gelée or tiny vegetables from the garden with possibly a curry-mayonnaise dip. In the city hors d'oeuvres were more elaborate. They might be little pieces of croque monsieur or unsalted blanched almonds or twisted cheese sticks or miniature quiches. Whatever they were, they had to be easy to eat with your hands.

In the summer because we had lobster pots in the bay, and everyone liked lobster very much, I made it a lot. When a lobster was for Madam and her friends, I would make Warm Lobster Salad with Basil Vinaigrette. If the children were home, I made Lobster Fra Diavolo, which they preferred. Madam always wanted her children to have what they wanted.

Warm Lobster Salad with Basil Vinaigrette

Serves 1

Obviously this can easily be multiplied for the number of people being served.

BASIL VINAIGRETTE

½ cup light olive oil

¼ cup fresh lemon juice

Salt and pepper to taste

10 basil leaves, cut into very fine strips

Blend together all the ingredients and set aside until the lobster is cooked.

COURT BOUILLON

2 carrots, sliced

2 stalks celery, sliced

1 onion, sliced

Bouquet garni consisting of thyme, parsley, a bay leaf, and peppercorns

Salt

Enough water to cover the lobster

Simmer all the ingredients together for half an hour.

JULIENNED VEGETABLES

⅓ cup julienned carrots

⅓ cup julienned turnips

⅓ cup julienned zucchini, green skin only

⅓ cup julienned celery

While the court bouillon is cooking, prepare the vegetables. The vegetables should all be cut into thin, thin strips about 3 inches long. Blanch, just until slightly cooked and still crisp, the carrots, turnips and zucchini. Add the celery. Set aside.

1 lobster

When the court bouillon has cooked, add a live lobster, preferably about 1½ pounds, and simmer for 15 minutes. Drain the lobster carefully and remove to a work surface. Cut off the claws and remove the meat. Split the lobster down its underside and remove the tail meat to a warm plate. Place the 2 pieces of tail meat, red side up, like parentheses, then stand the claw meat up between them facing front like little soldiers. Arrange the vegetables on both sides and spoon basil vinaigrette over the lobster meat.

If the lobster is small enough or I am serving several on a platter, I sometimes take the heads and use them for decoration at the front of the dish.

Serve at once.

LOBSTER FRA DIAVOLO can also be modified for the number of people to be served. What you need is one small lobster for each person. Cut it into pieces. For this the lobster has to be raw, but if you don't want to cut it up alive, you can bring a pot of water to a boil and dunk it, headfirst, into the boiling water until it is limp. Most of a lobster's nervous system is around the head, so this kills it without cooking it.

When the lobster is cut up, crack the shells to let the other tastes infuse the meat, then sauté the pieces in a little olive oil until they start to turn red. Add to the pan some crushed cloves of garlic and some oregano, lots of chopped onions (1 cup for each lobster), some stewed tomatoes, and parsley. Cover the pan and simmer for about 40 minutes. Keep the heat low because you don't want the meat to get too hard.

I think the children liked this because they could get pretty messy eating it with their nutcrackers and picks.

Oeufs en Gelée

Serves 6

ASPIC

4 cups chicken stock (see page 132)

4 envelopes (4 Tablespoons) unflavored gelatin

3 egg whites, lightly beaten

Combine all the ingredients in a saucepan and heat slowly, stirring constantly. When the mixture boils up in the pan, remove from the heat. At this point you can stir in 2 tablespoons of cognac if you like the taste.

Let stand for 10 minutes. While it is standing rinse a cheesecloth in cold water, wring it out, and use it to line a sieve. Pour the aspic through the lined sieve into a bowl. Refrigerate the bowl until the aspic begins to thicken a little.

Spoon a thin layer into the bottom of 6 egg molds or custard cups and chill. If the aspic has gotten too solid, it can be reheated and cooled again to the right consistency.

MOLDS

Leaves from 2 sprigs fresh tarragon or 2 thin slices black truffle

6 eggs, poached

6 thin slices ham

Watercress

Dip the tarragon leaves in the aspic and arrange them in a V in the bottom of each mold. If tarragon isn't available, make the Vs from slivers of truffle. Chill.

Trim the poached eggs and the ham to the size and shape of the molds. Place first an egg, yolk down, in each mold over the aspic, then cover it with a slice of ham. Fill the molds with chilled but still liquid aspic and return them to the refrigerator. Pour the remaining aspic into a shallow dish to make a layer about ½ inch thick and chill.

When the aspic is solid in both the molds and the dish, turn over the dish so the aspic falls out and cut decorative forms from it. You can use tiny aspic cutters available at good kitchenware stores or, if you have the skill, cut freehand. If the cutouts have to wait, return them to the refrigerator.

To unmold, dip each mold into a bowl of warm water and turn out onto an individual serving plate. Garnish with watercress and aspic cutouts.

POACHED STRIPED BASS OR RED SNAPPER

Serves 6 to 8

COURT BOUILLON

2 cups chopped onions
1 bay leaf
1 cup coarsely chopped parsley
2 cups coarsely chopped celery, leaves included
2 cups coarsely chopped leeks (both white and green parts)
Salt
10 black peppercorns
2 cups dry white wine
3 sprigs fresh thyme or 1 teaspoon dried
2 cloves garlic, peeled and cut in half

3½- to 5-pound striped bass or red snapper, cleaned, with gills removed and head and tail left on if possible

(continued on next page)

Combine all the ingredients for the court bouillon in a big pot with a gallon of water. Bring to a boil, lower the heat, and simmer for 15 minutes. Let cool, then pour through a coarse sieve into a fish poacher or any other pan long and deep enough to hold the fish flat covered with liquid.

If you are not using a fish poacher, wrap the fish in muslin to make it easier to get in and out of the liquid. Submerge the fish in the court bouillon. Bring to a boil, then reduce the heat and simmer for 15 minutes. Turn the heat off and let the fish stand in the bouillon for another half an hour or longer.

Remove the fish and carefully peel and pare away the skin. Arrange on a platter on a bed of parsley or, if you don't have it, Boston lettuce. Serve lukewarm or at room temperature, accompanied by the following nonspicy salsa.

SALSA

2 Tablespoons Dijon mustard
1 Tablespoon red wine vinegar
¼ cup olive oil
¼ cup corn oil
1 ripe tomato, peeled, seeded, and cubed
2 Tablespoons finely chopped shallots
1 Tablespoon finely chopped basil
1½ Tablespoons finely chopped parsley
Salt and pepper

Combine the mustard and vinegar in a small bowl and slowly whisk in the oils. Stir in the rest of the ingredients and serve at room temperature.

I always put a little bunch of parsley in the fish's mouth and spoon a little of the salsa over its peeled body so it looks appetizing.

Tarragon Chicken

Serves 4 to 6

This is a simple version of the classic Poulet à l'Estragon, one of the world's best chicken dishes. I only made this in the summer because it can't be made without fresh tarragon. But now that fresh herbs are available year-round, it can be served anytime.

4 Tablespoons chopped fresh tarragon leaves, divided
10 Tablespoons (1¼ sticks) butter, divided
Salt and pepper
1 (4-pound) roasting chicken
½ cup heavy cream

Work 2 tablespoons of the chopped tarragon leaves into 6 tablespoons of the butter. Season with salt and pepper, then stuff into the cavity of the chicken.

Melt 2 tablespoons of the remaining butter in a heavy ovenproof casserole that has a cover and is just large enough to hold the chicken comfortably. Place the bird on its side in the casserole and cook, covered, for about 45 minutes over medium heat. Then turn the chicken over onto the other side and baste with the tarragon butter that will have melted out of the cavity.

When the chicken is tender, about another 45 minutes, remove it to a serving dish. A flat platter won't work for this. Stir the remaining butter into the juices in the casserole. When the butter has melted, add the cream and the remaining 2 tablespoons of chopped tarragon. Bring to a boil, stirring, and when the sauce has thickened, pour it over the chicken and serve.

Vitello Tonnato

Serves 6 to 8

VEAL

1 (5-pound) loin of veal, rolled and tied, at room temperature
Salt and pepper
2 stalks celery, chopped
2 carrots, chopped
1 large onion, chopped

Preheat the oven to 400°.

Brush a roasting pan with a light film of oil. Season the meat with salt and pepper and place it in the pan. Surround it with the chopped vegetables. Put the pan in the oven and immediately turn the heat down to 375°. Roast for 40 minutes or until, when the veal is pricked with a fork, the juice runs just slightly pink.

Let the veal cool at room temperature, not refrigerated. While it cools, prepare the sauce.

TONNATO SAUCE

1 (7-ounce) can tuna packed in oil, drained
1 Tablespoon capers
4 cornichons, lightly chopped
1 Tablespoon chopped flat-leaf parsley
1 cup homemade mayonnaise (see page 82)
Juice from the veal

In a food processor, puree the tuna, capers, cornichons, and parsley until smooth and homogenized.

Thin the mayonnaise slightly with the veal juice, then add it to the puree. The amount of juice you will use will vary depending on how light you want the sauce to be.

To serve, slice the veal very thin and arrange it on a serving platter so the slices overlap slightly. Pour a little of the sauce over the veal on the platter, and pass the rest with it. This looks pretty garnished with capers and whole cornichons to give some nice green color to the pale meat with the pale sauce.

Tender Garden Vegetables

Serves 6 to 8

1 small cauliflower
1 head broccoli
4 carrots, peeled
4 zucchini
10 ounces (1½ to 2 cups) snow peas
10 ounces (1½ to 2 cups) string beans
1 teaspoon salt
¼ cup lemon juice
8 Tablespoons (1 stick) butter
Salt and white pepper to taste

Cut all excess stem off the cauliflower and broccoli so that only very small florets remain.

Cut the carrots and the zucchini into 2-inch lengths and then into a fine julienne.

Wash the snow peas, then string them by breaking off the stem end and pulling it and the string attached to it away. Discard the strings.

Wash the beans, then using a very sharp knife, cut the ends off, and slice the beans lengthwise into 4 strips.

(continued on next page)

Bring a large kettle of water to a boil. Add the teaspoon of salt. While it is coming to the boil, prepare a large bowl of very cold water.

Ladle 3 to 4 cups of the boiling water into a 2-quart saucepan. This is where you will blanch the vegetables. Place over heat and when the water in the saucepan returns to the boil, add the lemon juice and drop in the cauliflower florets. They should cook only briefly, so they retain their crispness. After about a minute, drain the florets and immediately plunge them into the cold water. Leave them there until they are completely cool, then remove from the water and drain thoroughly.

Pour out the cauliflower water. Refill the saucepan from the kettle and repeat blanching—omitting the lemon juice—with the broccoli, carrots, zucchini, snow peas, and the beans. Use fresh water from the kettle for each vegetable. The cooking time will vary, but none should be very long. The beans and snow peas, for instance, just go in and then out. Be especially careful not to overcook the broccoli.

Set the vegetables aside at room temperature until you are ready to serve. Then melt the butter in a pan large enough to hold all the vegetables and sauté them gently until they are heated through. Add salt and pepper to taste.

Blueberry Pie

On Martha's Vineyard there are lots of wild blueberry trees at the end of the property, and sometimes we go and pick buckets of them. It's far to go and you get scratched up, but when this pie is made with those little wild berries, it is really something. But it's great made with regular fresh berries too.

This is an example of the way I changed recipes as I got more confident about my cooking. When I found this recipe, I made it the way it said in the cookbook: with orange rind in the crust. I didn't like that flavor; I thought the orange took away from the taste of the blueberries, so now I make it with my own crust, which I prefer.

CRUST

2 cups flour
¼ teaspoon salt
2 teaspoons sugar
12 Tablespoons (1½ sticks) butter, cut into small pieces
Up to 5 Tablespoons ice water

Mix the flour, salt, and sugar together in a bowl, then cut the butter in with a pastry blender or 2 knives. Add a tablespoon of the water and mix it in before putting in the next tablespoon. Stop adding water as soon as the pastry can be formed into a ball. Divide it in half, wrap each piece in waxed paper, and refrigerate for 1 hour.

FILLING

1 cup sugar
1 Tablespoon cornstarch
½ teaspoon grated nutmeg
4 cups fresh blueberries
2 Tablespoons (¼ stick) butter, cut into small pieces

Confectioners' sugar

Preheat the oven to 375°.

Roll out half the pastry and use it to line a 9-inch pie pan.

Mix together the sugar, cornstarch, and the nutmeg, then sprinkle over the blueberries. Toss until the dry ingredients are evenly distributed. Spoon the filling into the pastry-lined pan and dot the top with the butter.

Roll out the remaining pastry and use it to cover the top of the pie. Moisten the edges

(continued on next page)

with water and seal the 2 crusts together. Trim off the extra dough, then cut a few slits in the top crust to allow the steam to escape.

Bake for 1 hour, then remove from the oven and let cool on a rack. When cool, sprinkle with confectioners' sugar.

Peach Ice Cream

Makes 3 to 4 quarts

8 cups heavy cream
1½ cups sugar
3 cups fresh peaches, peeled, seeded, and crushed
Juice of 2 lemons, strained

Scald the cream, then take the pan off the heat and stir in the sugar until it is dissolved. Stir in the peaches and any juice in the bowl, then the strained lemon juice.

Let cool, then freeze in an ice cream maker according to the manufacturer's instructions.

I tried adding a little peach brandy to this but decided I preferred the pure flavor. If you like, you can try it, but don't add too much or the alcohol could prevent the custard from freezing.

Iced Tea

Put either 6 tea bags or 6 tablespoons loose tea in a teaball or muslin in a deep mixing bowl with a nice bunch of fresh mint. Pour 6 cups boiling water over the tea and mint, cover, and let steep for 10 minutes. The tea should be strong because the melting ice will weaken it.

Add ⅔ of a cup of orange juice and ⅓ of a cup of lime juice, then pour through a strainer into a pitcher. Cover the pitcher with foil and refrigerate. Madam liked her tea with no sugar, but Caroline likes it a little sweet, so I add ½ cup of the sugar syrup to hers when I pour it out into a glass full of ice.

SUGAR SYRUP

Bring 1 cup water and 1 cup sugar to a boil together. When cool, store in a screw-top jar in the refrigerator.

July 28 on Martha's Vineyard.

7

JULY

Madam's Birthday on Skorpios

✵

When I first went to Skorpios, which was in 1970, the year after Madam got married, we lived on the boat because the houses being built on the island for us weren't finished. On the *Christina* we each had our bedroom with our own little living room, so it was fine.

Skorpios had belonged to four brothers, I think, but they were using it just for fishing. When Mr. Onassis first bought the island, he went there, but he usually stayed on the boat—or, I suppose, in The Pink House, which was there already. We called it The Pink House because it was painted pink and Mrs. Onassis liked that color. It was not a shocking pink but more a kind of very subdued color. That was her house. Sometimes guests stayed in The Pink House, and sometimes Madam and Mr. Onassis slept there, but they didn't live there. And sometimes we had lunch on the porch outside. Never dinner, as far as I remember. We had dinner either on the boat or in our house. But usually on the boat.

There were three houses: The Pink House, the Hill House where Madam and Mr. Onassis did live, and the house in the middle, where I stayed with the children. Our house sort of came around and connected the others, like a cloister with a garden in the middle. We each had our own little apartment: a room with a bathroom and a separate entrance.

Then there were little stone steps and you could go up to the Hill House or down to The Pink House.

When Madam first came she renewed The Pink House. There was this Italian architect Mongiardino, who had all the floors painted. I think they were stenciled. They were beautiful. Each room had a different design in pastel colors. Some were green, some were in the pink, some were with different colors, but absolutely extremely chic.

The bedrooms were all very simple because Madam liked plain things. The beds were all white, with nice colorful crocheted Greek bedspreads. And lots of pillows and muslin netting, that stuff for mosquitoes. The rugs were flokatis, and the furniture was plain wood: Greek furniture or Italian—country style but country chic. It was all very nice to look at, very relaxing, very easygoing.

Very early one morning on Skorpios, John, Anthony Radziwill, and I are waiting for the helicopter to take the boys to the Athens airport, where they were going to catch a plane to go to camp.

Madam always said you should live the way the people of the country live. So there was the same kind of furniture, maybe a little bit more refined because her taste was more refined, but we didn't try to have something that looked like a city apartment in a house on Skorpios. It was all comfortable and at the same time very country chic. All the houses were like this.

The island was beautiful, like a tropical island. It was pretty big, too; the compound covered just the tip. There was one road that ran all the way around the perimeter. You could walk around it, but it would take you a while.

You could drive the road in about twenty minutes. We each had a little jeep. Mine worked with a battery. It must have been a big battery, because I never had to recharge it. Maybe the garage staff did it at night when we were asleep. I don't know how it worked, but I loved my car. It was open—no doors, just a roof. Usually we were there in the summer, when you don't want to lock yourself in.

We also had a nice sailboat, the *Caroline,* which Mr. Onassis gave to Guess Who. It had about four bedrooms and a kitchen. Sometimes the children and I would use it to go on expeditions. We could sail to different islands and stay overnight. You could go with the sails or with the motor. Usually we liked to go with the sails at least for part of the trip.

The only problem on those trips was that nobody got any sleep. The children, usually at least four of them, wanted to sleep out on the deck. They would get all excited and play around instead of lying quietly. And I didn't dare close my eyes because I was afraid someone would fall off.

I remember once we went all the way over to the other Greek islands to visit. The children were young at that time and had a couple of cousins or friends with them. A captain had to go along because we wouldn't have known how to run the boat. And we had a cook with us and some others because it was before I cooked.

Our meals were prepared by Richard, the son of the butler on the *Christina.* He would take us around, and sometimes he was watching the children. They had fun with him. He was a young fellow, maybe at that time twenty, twenty-two. He was doing things with the children, but he came with us to cook. Fried eggs or something; I don't know what we ate. I think he was cooking pasta. We probably left with food for ten weeks and stayed only three days.

This is us cruising on the Caroline.

This snapshot of me on the deck of the Caroline *is the kind that has the date it was developed on it. So I know this was the summer of 1970, my first on Skorpios.*

We all loved just being on Skorpios, but the main event of July, wherever we were, was

Madam's birthday. Once I started to cook, I could make her a special meal, but before that, part of my birthday present to her was a play. The children were delighted, and she was delighted too.

Tina and Anthony Radziwill, Caroline and John singing, "Ark, ark, ark" on Christmas Eve 1969 in London.

The first year I came we had a Christmas pageant and sang Christmas carols. We were staying with the Radziwills in London, so I had the four children sing: Caroline and John, Anthony and Tina Radziwill. I think we did it Christmas Eve. I was just here for a few months, and my English wasn't too good. I know now the carol is "Hark, the Herald Angels Sing," but the way it sounded to me then was "Ark, Ark, Ark, the Angels Sing." So that's how I taught it to the children and how they were singing it until they figured out it was wrong. They still tease me about that, especially Caroline. "Ark, Ark, Ark."

I wrapped some white sheets around the children and I made crowns of laurel for their heads. Children like to get dressed up, even if it's only with a sheet. And they were singing for the family.

After that the children grew too old. Not John, really, because he was younger, but Anthony and Caroline were already thirteen or fourteen, and they didn't want to sing Christmas carols anymore.

But during the summer for Madam's birthday, we did a play. Her birthday was July 28, so we usually started preparing at the beginning of July. We had a month, but it wasn't a serious month. We really worked constantly maybe two, two and a half weeks.

Our play was usually a classic. We had several Molière plays, and one year, *Cyrano de Ber-*

JULY 28 1971 SKORPIOS

PROGRAM

you are invited tonight at 7:30
to THE IMAGINARY INVALID
BY MOLIERE
WITH
ARGAN – John Kennedy
Angélique – Tina Radziwill
Tounette – Elizabeth Campbell + Marta
Page – Colin Emlyn

Dear Dear Marta

You made my birthday so happy

And whatever you did with the fish tonight is

the most exquise thing I have ever tasted —

And your garniture of zucchini + tomatoes

makes me think we should have them on our big

night —

With so many thanks + so much love

J.

M.S.

J.K.O.

gerac. I could not keep the whole play, so I had to work on it and make a small play out of it. The classic play was there; I just rebuilt it. It was a lot of work to do because it had to make sense. You can't just take away sentences and add others.

Everything else was homemade as well. Nothing was prefabricated. Caroline made the programs. We usually didn't have any curtains because that was difficult. But we always had a stage: a rug, a table, all the accessories. For costumes we used Madam's skirts or blouses. We wrecked her closet that day. We took everything. But she was very willing.

Our reward was playing for Madam. She was so happy seeing her children onstage.

All this was before I started cooking. Once I was doing that I liked to give Madam a special meal on her day. The menu changed. In the early days I made vol-au-vent, either chicken or seafood. Later I made a rolled loin of veal, which was the same meal we had for Christmas.

Madam's birthday in The Pink House. Madam and Mr. Onassis are congratulating me on my performance as the soubrette in the birthday-present play. The first time Mr. Onassis saw me in one of the productions, he very shrewdly said, "You've done this before."

Truffle Soup

Serves 4

This was one of Madam's favorite soups. It should be prepared and served in four individual ovenproof tureens or bowls.

CHICKEN

5 ounces raw chicken breast meat

1 cup chicken stock (see page 132)

Poach the chicken breasts in the stock for 10 minutes, then cut them into ¼-inch dice.

MIREPOIX

1 teaspoon olive oil

5 Tablespoons finely minced, peeled carrots

2 Tablespoons finely minced celery

6 Tablespoons finely minced mushrooms, any kind

Salt and pepper

Thyme flowers

Coat the inside of a small saucepan with the olive oil and heat it. Add the diced carrots and cook, covered, over medium heat.

After 3 minutes add the diced celery.

After 6 more minutes add the mushrooms and cook another 3 minutes.

The vegetables should cook 9 minutes in all, covered. The idea is to have the vegetables give up their juices, not to brown. Add the salt and pepper and a pinch of thyme flowers.

(continued on next page)

SOUP AND SERVING

4 sheets phyllo pastry, available frozen in most supermarkets (or frozen puff pastry, which is less crumbly)
4 Tablespoons (½ stick) butter, melted
1 egg yolk, beaten

While the vegetables are cooking heat the oven to 450°.

Lay out one of the layers of pastry on a countertop. Use a pastry brush to paint it with melted butter. Fold the pastry in half and paint again, then do it one more time. Use a tureen as a pattern, and cut a circle of pastry the size of the top opening. Repeat with the other three pieces of pastry.

2 ounces canned black truffles, sliced very thin
2 Tablespoons Sauce Perigord, a truffle sauce, available at fancy food departments
The juice from the truffles
3 cups hot chicken stock (see page 132)

Place a spoonful of mirepoix vegetables into the bottom of each tureen. Add 1½ teaspoons of the truffle sauce, 1 teaspoon of the truffle juice, and a quarter of the diced chicken and the truffles. Add ¾ of a cup of chicken stock to each.

Brush the rims of the pastry circles with the egg yolk and press the pastry, yolk side down, over the tops of the tureens, using the egg to seal the edges tight.

Set the tureens on a jelly roll sheet and place them in the oven. They will cook very fast. The pastry will expand and turn golden and when that happens, they are done.

Serve at once. Guests should use their soup spoons to break the crust, which should fall into the soup.

When I first saw a recipe the instructions were to cover the bowls with foil, but I thought that wasn't elegant and came up with this. The aroma when you first break through that crust is amazing.

Chicken Vol-au-Vent

Serves 4 to 6

You could make your own pastry shell, but I prefer cooking to baking, so I had them made. Slice the shell horizontally but unevenly, about two or three inches down from the top, so that there is a sort of pastry bowl and then a lid.

VELOUTÉ SAUCE

8 Tablespoons (1 stick) butter
⅓ cup flour
3 cups chicken stock (see page 132)
½ teaspoon salt
White pepper

Melt the butter in a medium saucepan. Stir in the flour and keep cooking over medium heat, stirring constantly, until the roux becomes golden brown, about 10 minutes.

Little by little, stir in the stock. Keep adding and stirring until the sauce thickens. Add the salt and a little pepper and continue to cook, uncovered, stirring occasionally and skimming often, until the sauce is reduced to about 2½ cups and is thick and creamy.

FILLING

2 whole chicken breasts, poached, then cut into ½- to 1-inch pieces
1½ pounds wild mushrooms, chopped if larger than 1 inch or so
12-inch vol-au-vent shell
Chopped parsley

Fold the cut chicken and mushroom pieces into the warm sauce. Spoon into the shell, sprinkle with chopped parsley. Replace the top of the pastry, and serve right away.

One hint: It is hard for people to serve themselves this dish with the pastry lid, so I always cut it like a pie into servings. That way, everyone would get some of the crunch from the lid and the delicious sauce soaked into the base.

Chicken Stock

Makes 3 to 4 quarts

5 pounds chicken parts, a combination of bones, necks, and wings
2 onions, peeled and chopped
3 stalks celery with leaves, chopped
2 unpeeled carrots with tops, cut into chunks
2 leeks, green part only, coarsely chopped
5 sprigs fresh thyme or 2 teaspoons dried
2 sprigs fresh rosemary or 1 teaspoon dried
2 bay leaves
15 black peppercorns
6 sprigs parsley
1 large clove garlic, unpeeled

Rinse the chicken parts under cold running water. Place in a large kettle or stockpot. Add the rest of the ingredients and water to cover.

Bring to a boil, then immediately reduce the heat and skim the surface. Cover and simmer for 2½ hours, skimming occasionally.

Rinse a large piece of cheesecloth in cold water, wring it dry, then use it to line a large strainer or colander. Place the strainer over a clean pot and ladle in the stock. Press down on the bones and vegetables to get all their juices out.

Leave the strainer resting over the pot, cover the whole thing, and refrigerate until the stock is chilled. Remove the strainer and you will see that fat has risen and congealed on the top of the stock. Skim it off and discard, then store the stock in quart or pint containers so it will be available when you want it.

This can stay in the refrigerator for a day or so, but if it stays longer, it should be brought to a boil each day to kill any germs. An easier way to store stock is to freeze it.

ROAST LOIN OF VEAL WITH MOREL MOUSSE

Serves 10

You will need to find a really good butcher to butterfly the veal the right way. Before I found the right place, I used to have to send the roast back two times sometimes. You have to pay, but it has to be right. When the butcher has butterflied the loin, he will return to you the pieces he trimmed. These can be used to make the mousse.

This recipe is usually made with sweetbreads in the mousse, but Madam didn't care for them, so I had to experiment. We both liked this better.

MOREL MOUSSE

About 12 ounces (more or less) veal tenderloin, ground
1 shallot, finely chopped
6 dried morels, soaked, rinsed, and patted dry
½ teaspoon salt
Pinch of white pepper
1 egg white
¼ cup heavy cream

(continued on next page)

Place the veal, shallot, and morels in the bowl of a food processor and turn the machine on and off quickly two or three times to blend them. Add salt and pepper then the egg white and cream and turn the machine on and off the same way a few more times, until the mixture is smooth. You want it really moussey. Transfer to a bowl, cover, and refrigerate until you need it.

LOIN OF VEAL

A 3-pound eye of veal loin, completely trimmed and butterflied
1 teaspoon salt
½ teaspoon white pepper
10 large spinach leaves, washed and dried
½ cup coarsely chopped small white turnips
½ cup coarsely chopped onions
½ cup coarsely chopped carrots
2 cloves garlic, crushed

SAUCE

1 ounce dried morels, soaked overnight in 1 cup water
1 cup dry white wine
1½ to 2 cups veal or chicken stock (see page 132)
1 teaspoon butter
2 shallots, chopped fine
1 cup heavy cream

Preheat the oven to 450°.

Open the veal out flat on the counter, and season the inside with the salt and pepper. Lay 5 large spinach leaves down the natural crease along the center of the veal. Spread the mousse over the spinach, making sure that the mousse covers only the middle section of the loin. Cover the mousse with the remaining spinach so it is completely encased in spinach.

(continued on page 136)

Roll the loin up carefully so the mousse stays in place, then tie kitchen string around the roll every 2 inches or so.

Place the veal in a roasting pan and roast for 20 minutes, then remove it from the oven and lower the temperature to 375°. Lift the veal out of the pan and scatter the turnips, onions, carrots, and garlic in the bottom of the pan. Replace the veal on top of the vegetables, return to the oven, and roast another 25 to 30 minutes.

While the meat is roasting, drain the morels through a double layer of cheesecloth. Save the liquid they were soaking in. Wash the mushrooms well and set them aside.

Remove the meat from the oven and keep it warm on a platter. Leave the vegetables in the roasting pan.

Put the roasting pan with the vegetables still in it over a burner. Pour in the white wine, and over low heat, use a wooden spoon to scrape up all the little pieces of meat and vegetables stuck to the pan.

Scrape the contents of the pan into a saucepan—with the cooked vegetables, too. Add 1½ cups of the stock and the reserved morel soaking water. If that looks skimpy, add more stock. Cook over high heat until the liquid is reduced to about 2 cups. Strain it through a fine sieve, discard the vegetables, and set the sauce base aside.

Melt the butter in a heavy saucepan and lightly sauté the shallots. Add the morels and the cream, stirring over low heat until thickened. Stir constantly to keep the mixture smooth, as you slowly add the sauce base. Serve immediately with the sliced veal.

Lori Walther, the food stylist for the photographs in this book, made this recipe perfectly. When we were cleaning up after, she suggested that the sauce would be wonderful by itself on pasta. I've tried it and she was right.

Rosemary Potatoes

Serves 12

If you use medium-sized potatoes, you can probably get about four balls out of each. I either make little balls about the size of marbles with a melon baller, or I use a knife and pare the potatoes into olive shapes. There is an olive-shaped baller, but I haven't used one. If you do use a baller though, you can leave the potatoes unpeeled, so that they are red on the top and white on the bottom. When they are cooked, they look like cute little mushrooms. If you can get tiny red new potatoes small enough, naturally you can use them whole, but those are really hard to find.

You don't have to clarify the butter, but it makes the dish look prettier and it ensures it won't burn.

6 pounds red potatoes
10 Tablespoons (1¼ sticks) butter, clarified
1 Tablespoon chopped fresh rosemary
Salt and pepper

Preheat the oven to 400°.

Peel the potatoes and cut them into pieces the size and shape of olives or into little balls. See note above.

Toss the potatoes with the butter in an ovenproof pan, then roast for 15 minutes. Remove from the oven and sprinkle with the rosemary.

Return to the oven and roast an additional 35 minutes or until the potatoes can be pierced easily with a fork. Toss lightly with salt and pepper and serve very hot.

One of the birthday cakes I made for Madam.

My cooking to please people started with a cake. That's funny, because even today I don't really like to bake. I prefer to make real food. But I always make some sort of cake for birthdays. There has to be one. There have to be candles to blow out. Everyone in the family likes chocolate, so I make a white or yellow or chocolate cake—it doesn't matter as long as there is chocolate icing.

Mr. Onassis really loved chocolate cake. Mrs. Onassis did too. So, every day, every meal, there was a chocolate cake baked in case anyone wanted some along with another dessert.

Well, I said to myself at one point, when Mr. Onassis comes back to New York, I'm going to bake him a chocolate cake to make him happy. I had no clue how to bake a cake, so to be sure that I wasn't missing anything, I bought a Duncan Hines mix.

I baked the cake and it was really terrific. You can't miss with that mix. That evening I told Charlie, the butler, When you serve the dessert, serve the cake. So he did, and a little later he came to fetch me. "Mr. Onassis would like to see you," he said. "It's about the chocolate cake."

When I went into the dining room, Mr. Onassis was really smiling. "This is the most wonderful cake I ever ate! How did you do it? I want you to give me the recipe for my chef."

I never planned to tell him how I did the cake but I couldn't produce a recipe so I had to tell him I made it out of a mix. Duncan Hines. American food. He said, "I don't care. It's so good and I love it."

So from that time on we kept shipping boxes of Duncan Hines chocolate cake mix to the house in France and to the boat. The chef, Clement, got very upset. He told me, "This is the first time in my life I have had to cook with powder! I can't cook with powder."

When Mr. Onassis heard, he just said, "I don't care. That is the chocolate cake I like."

So from that time on, we had the Duncan Hines chocolate cake with every meal.

Since then, I have learned to bake a little more.

White Butter Cake

6 Tablespoons (¾ stick) butter, at room temperature
¾ cup sugar
1 cup flour
1 teaspoon baking powder
Pinch of salt
3 egg whites from "large" eggs
⅓ cup milk
1 teaspoon vanilla

(continued on next page)

Preheat the oven to 350°. Butter a 9-inch cake pan. Line the bottom with a piece of waxed paper cut to fit. Butter the paper and sprinkle with flour. Shake pan to distribute the flour evenly and get rid of the excess.

In a large bowl, beat the butter and sugar until light and fluffy.

In another bowl, stir the flour, baking powder, and salt together and set aside.

In yet another bowl, combine the egg whites, milk, and vanilla.

Beat one-third of the dry ingredients into the butter/sugar mixture. When they are incorporated, beat in half the liquid mixture until that is incorporated. Continue adding and beating in the same order: dry, liquid, dry.

When all the ingredients are incorporated, pour the batter into the prepared pan and smooth the top. Bake 25 to 30 minutes or until a toothpick poked into the center of the cake comes out clean.

Let the cake cool in the pan on a rack for 5 minutes, then turn it out onto the rack, peel off the paper, and let cool completely.

Slice the cake into 2 layers and frost.

Yellow Birthday Cake

16 Tablespoons (2 sticks) butter

2 cups sugar

4 eggs

4 cups flour, sifted

½ teaspoon salt

2 Tablespoons baking powder

1 cup milk

1 teaspoon vanilla

Preheat the oven to 350°. Butter and flour two 9-inch cake pans.

In a large bowl, beat the butter and sugar together until they are light. Beat in the eggs, one at a time. In another bowl, sift together the dry ingredients and add one-third to the butter mixture, beating well. Add half of the milk. Continue to add the dry ingredients, alternating with the milk, 5 additions in all. Stir in the vanilla and blend well.

Pour the batter evenly into the 2 prepared pans. Bake for 45 minutes, then cool on racks.

Chocolate Birthday Cake

1 cup milk, divided
4 ounces semisweet chocolate, grated
8 Tablespoons (1 stick) butter
1½ cups sugar
3 eggs
1 teaspoon baking soda
2 cups flour
1½ teaspoons baking powder
1 teaspoon vanilla

Preheat the oven to 350°. Butter and flour two 9-inch pans.

Pour ½ cup of the milk into a saucepan, add the grated chocolate, and bring to a boil. Set aside to cool.

In a large bowl, beat the butter until light and fluffy, then beat in the sugar thoroughly. Separate the eggs, putting the whites into a mixing bowl and beating the yolks, one at a

(continued on next page)

time, into the butter/sugar mixture. Stir the baking soda into the remaining ½ cup of milk. When it has fizzed a little, stir it into the butter mixture too.

Sift the flour and baking powder together.

Beat the egg whites until they hold stiff peaks, then fold the egg whites, alternately with the sifted ingredients, into the butter mixture. Don't overmix but make sure each addition is completely folded in before adding the next. When everything is completely folded in stir the vanilla into the chocolate milk and then fold that into the batter.

Pour half the batter into each of the 2 prepared pans. Bake for 30 minutes or until the tops, when pressed lightly, spring back.

Chocolate Frosting

7 ounces unsweetened chocolate
4 Tablespoons (½ stick) butter
2½ cups confectioners' sugar
3 Tablespoons milk
Dash of vanilla

Melt the chocolate in a saucepan over low heat. Add the butter and let it melt and simmer for about 1 minute. Sift in the confectioners' sugar and stir to mix, then add the milk, stirring constantly.

Let simmer for 5 minutes, stirring occasionally, then remove from the heat and stir in a few drops of vanilla. Let the frosting cool before using it.

Madam looks more delighted to see John than her birthday cake. Once the cake is in I can relax too. Grand Jackie celebrating her birthday with Caroline and her three children. This must have been July 29, the day after Madam's birthday party, when the dessert for lunch out on the terrace was leftover birthday cake

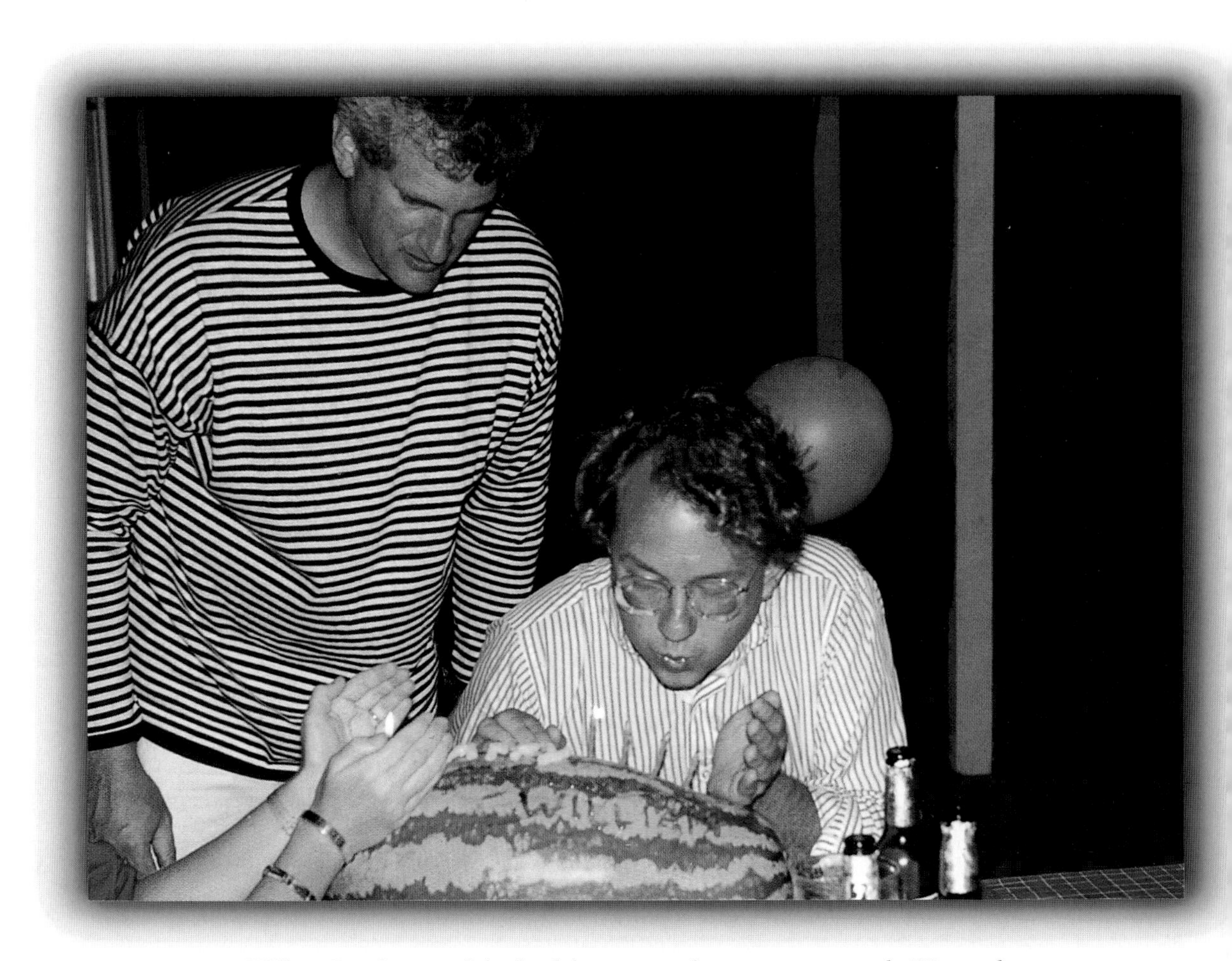

William Ivey Long with his birthday watermelon at our party on the Vineyard.

AUGUST

A Summer Birthday Party

This must have been in 1987—I know it was in August, when Mrs. Onassis was visiting her mother in Newport. There was a small group of about eight in the house on the Vineyard. Caroline and Ed, and John and their cousin Anthony Radziwill were there and some other friends.

One of the guests was William Ivey Long, a friend of Caroline's who has gone on to win awards for his costume designs. He was invited for the weekend, and it was his birthday, August 30, so we decided to make him a birthday party. We thought it would be more fun if we ate outside instead of inside in the dining room. But there were no lights on the patio. Usually the only meal outside was lunch. Dinner was always in the dining room.

Normally, when we sat outside, we put out those tall hurricane lamps—glass and inside there were candles. But there wasn't enough space on the table, and we wanted to do something different. So Efigénio, the butler, who is very handy, brought extension cords from inside, and rigged them up on the grape trellis, and we put some lights up there. We didn't put any covers on the lights, just bulbs so you could see what you were doing on the table. Madam wouldn't have liked those lights if she saw them. She probably would have thought we were gypsies. But by the following day everything was clean and put away.

It was kind of hectic. We all chipped in with the cooking and we all ate together. Everybody was swimming all day and boating and water-skiing, so at night the activities were more quiet because everybody was tired. They were knocked down by the sun. It wasn't really a party; it was just a birthday meal.

Because everyone was hungry after all the exercise, I served a first course of soup. We ate a lot of simple chowders in the summer, especially if it was a little cool at night.

We had a big watermelon for dessert and wrote "Happy Birthday William" on it instead of a cake. Then we sliced it on top of the table. I remember that watermelon because it looked so summery and it was a warm evening and we were just outside, horsing around. It was nice. Then we all had strawberry shortcakes, and I did put a candle on William's shortcake. It was a fun kids' party—very relaxed and casual.

If it had been a party for a friend of Mrs. Onassis I don't think we would have done it outside. I think we would have done it inside, in the dining room. Quietly. Not that it would have been quiet—that was a happy house, a happy home—but we would have used more of the things there. We wouldn't have made things up, like we did with the lights outside. We might have served somewhat lighter food, maybe seafood, which Madam liked very much. The meal would have been more normal. Doing things another way made the party more fun. Or maybe it was just different because it was a bunch of kids and they liked to laugh and be silly.

The way we lived on the Vineyard was not very formal anyway. For instance we always set the tables, indoors and outdoors, with country things. It was like the houses on Skorpios: Madam didn't want anything that looked too city for the country. We used blue and white cotton or linen because Madam liked the way that looked for tablecloths, napkins, place mats, everything. And she liked to collect antique serving bowls so we had a lot of them. You can see in the pictures that at William's party there were bottles all over the table. That wouldn't

My picture of the dead vines and the living grapes after Hurricane Bob.

have been if Madam was there. But the glasses we used weren't so fancy. What she liked were the Simon Pearce big goblets. They are hand blown, but not light crystal—sturdy glass. And we used the same goblets for water and for wine.

That arbor where we put the lights was for Concord grapes. When we had Hurricane Bob in August of 1991, it destroyed all the leaves but left the grapes still there. The leaves were all beat up and became brown very quickly, then they all fell off. But the grapes were still nice and green, and they got ripe the end of October, as usual. I remember because the caretaker's wife always makes grape jelly.

Corn Chowder

Serves 4 to 6

This can also be made with tomatoes or carrots instead of corn.

10 large ears of corn, cooked and with the kernels cut off. (Ten ears will yield about 4 cups kernels, which is what you'll need. Or use 2 [15-ounce] cans of kernels [about 4 cups]—it has to be canned, not frozen, and regular, not creamed.)
1 medium onion, finely chopped
2 cups water
2 cups milk
Salt and pepper
Chopped parsley

Combine all the ingredients in a large pot, bring to a boil, then reduce to a simmer and cook for 30 to 35 minutes.

Put the soup through a food mill with a coarse blade, or through a coarse sieve, or whirl one round in a food processor. You want to leave some whole kernels.

Just before serving, reheat and serve very hot, topped with chopped parsley.

Marinated Swordfish

Serves 6

This is a delicious dish, but because swordfish are almost becoming an endangered species there is a year's ban on eating them. So, please, don't try this recipe until that year is over.

This tastes best if you use harpooned swordfish. The flesh is sweeter. Ask your fish man if he can supply you. If you can't find harpooned fish, any good fresh netted swordfish will do.

2½ pounds swordfish, ¾ inch thick, preferably in 1 piece
Freshly ground pepper
4 Tablespoons (½ stick) butter, cut into small pieces
3 Tablespoons fresh chives, chopped
2 Tablespoons fresh basil, chopped
1 Tablespoon fresh oregano, chopped
1 Tablespoon fresh dill, chopped
2 Tablespoons fresh, flat-leafed parsley, chopped
½ cup light soy sauce

(continued on next page)

Several hours before you want to serve the fish, place it in an ovenproof baking dish, season with fresh pepper, and dot with butter. Sprinkle with the chopped herbs and pour the soy sauce over the top. Cover with plastic wrap and refrigerate.

One hour before you are going to cook it, remove the fish from the refrigerator and let it stand at room temperature.

Heat the broiler, then place the fish in the marinade, under it. Broil on one side only for about 10 minutes, basting often to keep the fish moist. It is ready when the skin around the outside pulls away from the flesh easily.

Jack's Mashed Potatoes

Serves 6

This is the recipe Jack asked me to put in the book for him. He also asked me to demonstrate how to make them for his class of four-year-olds. Jack had been bragging that I was the best cook in the world, and when the class tasted the potatoes they acted like they agreed.

5 pounds potatoes, any all-purpose white or yellow type
16 Tablespoons (2 sticks) butter, divided
4 cups milk, hot
Salt and pepper

Peel the potatoes, and place them in a large pot, with water to cover. Boil them for 40 minutes or so until they are very soft. They are ready if they fall apart when poked with a fork. Drain.

Off the heat, put 1½ sticks of the butter into the pot in which the potatoes were boiled. When it begins to melt from the heat of the pot, fit a food mill with a fine blade over the pot and put the potatoes through it. They really have to be milled; if they are actually mashed, they'll be lumpy.

Put the pot of potatoes back on the stove over *very* low heat. Stir with a whisk to incorporate the butter. Little by little, begin pouring in the hot milk. Stir a lot as you pour so the potatoes get really fluffy. You may not need all the milk; add enough so the potatoes get to the consistency of thick whipped cream.

This is a lot of work, and you have to stay over the stove whipping, but the finished result is worth it. Keep the potatoes over low heat and keep stirring. They have to be really stretched. If they get too thick, whisk in more milk.

Just before serving, beat in the remaining half stick of butter and salt and pepper to taste.

Pattypan Squash with Onions

Serves 6

8 Tablespoons (1 stick) butter
5 large onions, cut in half, then sliced medium thick
4 pounds squash; these should be tiny, about the size of a quarter. (If they are that small, leave them whole. If they are the size of a golf ball, halve them. Any larger, slice about 1 inch thick.)
Salt and pepper

Melt the butter in a large saucepan, and cook the onions until they are golden but not browned. Add the squash, and salt and pepper, and stir so everything gets mixed together.

Cover to keep the moisture in and cook for about 5 minutes, then remove the cover and cook another 30 minutes or so, until the squash is tender.

Sautéed Scallops Provençal

Serves 4

When Madam was on the Vineyard, she loved the local scallops. They were so sweet. I came up with several recipes for using them. This is Bunny Mellon's favorite. She always asked for it when she came.

SCALLOPS

1½ pounds bay scallops
1 medium lemon
Salt and pepper

CLARIFIED GARLIC BUTTER

8 Tablespoons (1 stick) unsalted butter
1 teaspoon finely chopped garlic

TOMATO FONDUE

5 firm ripe tomatoes
1 teaspoon salt
1 grind of pepper
Pinch of sugar
1 Tablespoon minced fresh basil
2 Tablespoons butter

TO COOK AND SERVE

½ cup flour
6 to 8 Tablespoons olive oil
3 Tablespoons finely chopped flat-leaf parsley
Lemon quarters

Wash the scallops under cold running water and dry on paper towels. Squeeze the juice of the lemon over them, sprinkle with salt and pepper, and let them rest while you prepare the clarified butter and the fondue.

To clarify the butter, first cut it into small pieces and put the pieces in an 8-inch frying pan. If you don't have one that small, use a small saucepan. Melt the butter over medium-low heat, being careful not to let it brown. You will do that later. Remove the pan from the heat and, using a spoon, skim all the foam off the top of the butter. Then tilt the pan and use a clean metal spoon to ladle out as much of the clear butter as you can into a small bowl. Leave behind the milky solids that will have settled to the bottom. Throw those away.

Wash and dry the pan, then return the clarified butter to it and put it over low heat. Cook the butter slowly until it begins to turn a light brown and smell nutty. Remove the pan from the heat and stir the teaspoon of minced garlic into the butter. The heat from the butter should be sufficient to cook the garlic. Set aside.

To make the tomato fondue, first bring a medium pan of water to a boil. Have ready a large bowl of very cold water. One by one, drop the tomatoes into the boiling water, then count to ten slowly, and remove the tomato with a slotted spoon and plunge it into the cold water. The peel should slip off. If it doesn't, return the tomato to the boiling water for a few more seconds. Cut the peeled tomatoes into quarters and scoop out the seeds. Then slice the tomatoes into ¼-inch strips, pat them dry with a paper towel, and toss them in a bowl with the salt, pepper, sugar, and basil.

Melt 2 tablespoons butter in a medium-sized, heavy frying pan over moderate heat. Add the tomatoes and, stirring constantly with a wooden spoon, cook them briskly for about 5 minutes. Shake the pan from time to time to make sure the tomatoes don't stick. When they are soft but not disintegrating, turn up the heat and boil rapidly until almost all the liquid in the pan has evaporated. Keep a careful eye on this process and don't take it too far or you will have a tomato puree, which is not your intention here. Remove the pan

(continued on next page)

from the heat while the tomato strips still retain some shape. Taste for seasonings, cover, and set the pan aside to be reheated when you are ready to serve the scallops.

Plan to start cooking the scallops 15 minutes before you want to serve them. Begin reheating the clarified butter and the fondue. Have an ovenproof serving platter heating. Sift the flour onto a strip of waxed paper and roll the scallops in the flour until they are coated. Shake off any excess.

Heat the olive oil in a large skillet. When it begins to smoke, arrange the scallops in the pan. Don't crowd them; the more room you have to turn them the better. Sauté for about 4 minutes on one side, then 3 minutes on the other. Adjust the heat so the scallops cook as quickly as possible without burning. If you think it needs it, add a little more oil to the skillet.

As the scallops are done, remove them to the waiting serving platter, mounding them in its center. If dinner is delayed for some reason, you can keep them warm, covered, in a very slow oven with the door ajar for 10 minutes, but no longer.

Before you bring the scallops to the table, pour the clarified butter over them and sprinkle them heavily with chopped parsley. Spoon the hot tomato fondue around the outside of the platter and decorate the rim with lemon quarters. If you want to be fancy, wrap the lemon quarters in gauze so they won't squirt.

This is a complete meal served with a salad and dessert. There is no need for another vegetable because the tomatoes serve that function. And because both the scallops and the tomatoes have their own liquid, anything else would have to be served on a separate plate, and would be awkward.

Sautéed Bay Scallops with Chives

Serves 4

½ sweet red bell pepper
10 Tablespoons (1¼ sticks) butter, clarified (see pages 152–53)
1 pound bay scallops
Pinch of ground cloves
3 Tablespoons finely chopped chives

Cut the pepper into strips, then dice it finely.

Heat half of the clarified butter in a sauté pan, and add the pepper, and cook for 2 minutes. Remove the pepper with a slotted spoon and set it aside.

Add the rest of the butter to the pan and sauté the scallops for 3 minutes, just until they are heated through. Sprinkle with the cloves, then stir in the peppers and the chives.

Serve on warmed plates.

Strawberry Shortcake

Serves 8

STRAWBERRIES

6 cups strawberries, hulled

1 cup sugar

SHORTCAKES

2 cups flour

4 teaspoons baking powder

1 teaspoon salt

1½ Tablespoons sugar

5 Tablespoons (⅔ stick) butter

⅔ cup milk

TOPPING

1 cup heavy cream

In a bowl, mash the strawberries with the back of a fork. Mash in the sugar and leave to marinate for several hours.

Preheat the oven to 375°.

To make the shortcakes, mix together the flour, baking powder, salt, and sugar in a large bowl. Cut the butter into small bits, then, using a pastry blender or 2 knives, cut the butter into the flour mixture until the result resembles coarse meal.

Slowly begin stirring in the milk. Use just enough to hold the dough together.

Turn the dough out onto a floured surface and knead for about 2 minutes. Form it into a roll about 8 inches long, then, using a sharp knife, slice the roll into 8 rounds, each 1 inch thick. Arrange the rounds on an ungreased cookie sheet and bake 10 to 12 minutes or until lightly browned.

Beat the cream until it holds soft peaks.

While the cakes are still warm, use a fork to split each in half around the equator. Arrange each bottom half on a round individual serving plate. Spread with some of the crushed marinated strawberries, then put the tops back on. Spread the rest of the strawberries over the tops, then cover with whipped cream.

You can, of course, make one big shortcake, and you could sweeten the whipped cream, and you could serve it on the side. But I always made individual cakes, and we thought there was enough sugar in the cakes and the strawberries. And Madam liked these really juicy, with the cream on top.

This is Rose, helping me shell peas.

9

SEPTEMBER

Family Favorites

Every year during the winter, Madam would get out the garden books and we would begin planning. We wanted a garden that would supply vegetables for us all summer. So we were taking into account Madam's taste, what was in favorite recipes, and when things got ripe. We were on the Vineyard from Memorial Day to more or less Labor Day, so that was when things should be available.

When we moved in, the land had never been gardened before, and it was very sandy, so the early years were sort of experiments. We did get strawberries and raspberries right the first year, but generally it needs a few years to get the ground into good shape. Once it was, Madam would tell Bert, who kept the garden, what we wanted and he would plant as early as possible so that when we first came we had a few early vegetables and lettuce. Other crops came when they came, but then Bert would plant again every few weeks so there was always a new crop of vegetables.

The garden wasn't that enormous, so I would try to save up Madam's favorites for her. She loved peas and she loved to eat them raw. If I was shelling them when she came into the kitchen, she would eat them all from the bowl before I was finished. We had maybe two rows of peas in the garden, so if I knew Madam was coming for the weekend, I would save the peas all week so she could have a good portion.

At first we wanted to grow everything we would eat but after trying it we decided some things weren't worth it. Potatoes took up too much room and didn't really taste different if they were home grown. We tried growing our own corn, but the ground wasn't very good for it and it never did too well and was too much work. Anyway, there was all that available at the farm stands, so we could get it very fresh.

What we finally ended up growing was the usual. We had green beans and haricots verts, yellow squash, zucchini, pattypan squash, and peas, carrots, cucumbers, eggplant, green peppers, beets, and radishes. And three different kinds of lettuce: leaf and head lettuce and arugula and herbs like dill for salads. Madam introduced Bert to Vidalia onions and he really liked them, so now he grows lots.

We sort of planned meals around what vegetable was good then. When President and Mrs. Clinton came for dinner, there were the tiny pattypan squashes so I made them the same meal I did for William Ivey Long's birthday because it was a favorite and everyone asked for it. I didn't know then about the President's milk intolerance or I might not have had mashed potatoes. But he ate them.

While I was cooking dinner for them there was a Secret Service man whose job was to sit in the kitchen and watch me. After a few minutes he said he could see I was fine, and then we just chatted.

The Clintons had visited before, but just for tea. We had a big bowl of white peaches, and they loved them and asked where such peaches came from. They were from the island, but the Clintons had never seen them before. And I made my Lemon Pound Cake. I knew the President liked sweets so we had that even though usually if we had tea it wasn't sweet. It was little sandwiches and crudités. Those were there too, but we wanted a sweet that wouldn't be gooey, and the pound cake was a big success. The Clintons wrote me very nice notes afterward.

During the summer when there were guests, we often served corn as a first course. Just fresh corn dropped right into the boiling water. There isn't anything better. The only thing

I had to watch for was not to let the menus get too starchy, because even though corn is a vegetable, it is also starch. The President's meal was like that. Corn and mashed potatoes would be too much.

Mrs. Clinton once came for lunch with Madam in the city, and they ate Oeufs Toupinel on trays in the study. I remember that because Madam specially asked me to make them because she thought Mrs. Clinton would like them.

Madam always tried to think of a food her guests would particularly enjoy—like Mrs. Vreeland and her Shepherd's Pie. Even in her play, *Full Gallop,* it talks about how all she ate was Shepherd's Pie.

Madam and I tried to keep a little book with guest lists and what was served and any special comments and recipes. We would start every year with a new book; they were bound in pretty cloth and the pages were blank. And at the beginning of the year, we would be really good and write everything down, but then things would get busy and we didn't write as much and then it would be another new year and we would make a big effort again.

Madam took this picture of me taking a picture of the kids.

The season at the Vineyard always ended with the big Labor Day cookout on the beach. Then we had to go back to New York and city life. I usually stayed a little later, four or five

days, to close the house the way I wanted. It was always sad to close the house for the season.

But sometimes Labor Day came a little later and we could squeeze in a few more days before we had to leave. Those felt like special family days, so we usually didn't have guests and just indulged ourselves. I always tried to cook everybody's favorites, and we ate lots of corn because we wouldn't be getting it so good again until next year.

Here I am happily surrounded by Ed and John at a family dinner.

I still have a hard time making myself walk like a lady. Madam took this. She was leaving and already in the car, when I remembered she'd left some flowers behind and rushed in to get them for her.

Rose's Vegetable Soup

Serves 6

¼ cup olive oil
2 bunches scallions (white parts only), chopped
3 medium zucchini
7 medium carrots, peeled
4 plum tomatoes, peeled and seeded
5 medium potatoes, peeled
Salt and pepper
6 cups chicken stock (page 132)
10 ounces fresh spinach, stems removed and cut or torn into pieces

Pour the olive oil into a large heavy-bottomed kettle. Add the chopped scallions, cover, and cook over low heat until soft and tender.

While the scallions are cooking, prepare the other vegetables. Cut the zucchini, carrots, tomatoes, and potatoes into small (about 1-inch) cubes. When the scallions are tender, add the rest of the vegetables, season to taste, and stir to combine. Cook for 5 minutes so the juices blend.

Add the stock and simmer the soup until the vegetables are tender, about 1 hour. Add the spinach pieces for the last 2 minutes of cooking. Allow to cool a little, then scoop out 1 cup and set it aside. Puree the rest of the soup in the blender. When you reheat the soup, return that unblended cup so there will be little chunks of vegetables in the soup when it is served.

I always have some freshly grated Parmesan cheese on the table; some use it and some don't.

This is a general recipe. It can be changed according to what vegetables are available and to cater to individual likes and dislikes. For instance, the last time I made this I found some fresh baby lima beans and put them in and they gave a wonderful taste and added some starch.

⁂

I have my own special way of making FRENCH FRIES. They come out soft and nice in the middle and with a great crunchy crust. I made them for the kids all the time, and Madam loved them too.

I use small red potatoes and cut off the round edges so they are little blocks, then I quarter them so they are small cubes. I cook them in hot Mazola or canola oil, of course fresh each time. I heat the oil, then drop the potatoes into it and cover the pan for 2 or 3 minutes. It's sort of like parboiling. But if they stay covered too long, they disintegrate, so they should just sort of steam.

Then I remove the lid and continue to cook until the potatoes get nice and brown. When they are done, I spread them on a jelly roll pan lined with paper towels so the fat is taken away. Then I salt them and serve them immediately.

⁂

Scrod Stew

Serves 4

1/8 teaspoon saffron threads
2 pounds scrod fillets
8 Tablespoons (1 stick) butter
1 medium onion, chopped
1 clove garlic, minced
3 large plum tomatoes, seeded and chopped
2 medium potatoes, peeled and diced
1 Tablespoon minced chervil
1 Tablespoon minced tarragon
Salt and white pepper
2 cups dry white wine
1 cup fish stock or bottled clam juice
1/2 cup chopped flat-leaf parsley

Sprinkle the saffron threads over a little hot water and set aside. Cut the fish into 2-inch chunks.

Melt the butter in a large skillet, then add onions and garlic and sauté until the onions are limp and golden. Add the tomatoes, potatoes, herbs, and salt and white pepper to taste. Cook, stirring, for 5 minutes.

Pour in the saffron threads in their water and stir; add the scrod, the wine, and the stock or juice. Partially cover the pot and simmer over low heat for 15 minutes.

The stew can be served now, but this is one dish I recommend making ahead of time and reheating because the second simmering brings out the flavors. If you are not going to serve it right away, cover and refrigerate it.

When you are ready to serve the stew, reheat and serve in deep bowls topped with chopped parsley.

Tatiana's Meatballs and Tomato Sauce

Serves 8

TOMATO SAUCE

½ cup olive oil

1 large onion, chopped

5 cloves garlic, peeled but left whole

6 pounds plum tomatoes

Salt and pepper

1 teaspoon sugar

¼ cup chopped fresh oregano

½ cup chopped fresh basil

Pour the olive oil into a heavy-bottomed 6-quart saucepan or Dutch oven. Add the onions, cover, and cook slowly until onions are golden brown. Add the garlic, re-cover, and cook another 2 minutes.

Peel the tomatoes by plunging them into boiling water for a slow count of 10, then draining them in a colander. The skins should slide off. Chop the peeled tomatoes roughly and add them to the pan.

Mix in the rest of the ingredients well and cook, uncovered, over low heat, stirring often, for at least 2 hours or until the sauce is nice and thick. The main thing is that this sauce not be watery, so cook as long as necessary to thicken it.

MEATBALLS

2 pounds ground beef

1 egg

1 garlic clove, crushed

¼ cup chopped parsley
6 slices good-quality white bread (Pepperidge Farm or Arnold), soaked in milk
Salt and pepper

If I'm making the meatballs for children, I use garlic salt instead of the garlic clove and leave out the salt. The taste of garlic can be sharp, and sometimes children prefer the milder garlic salt.

In a bowl, mix together the meat, egg, garlic, and parsley. Squeeze the milk out of the bread and add the bread to the meat mixture. Add salt and pepper to taste (see above) and combine well.

In a deep skillet, bring water about 3 inches deep to a boil.

Remove about 2 tablespoons of the meat mixture from the bowl and roll it between your hands to form a ball about the size of a golf ball or maybe a little bigger. Continue until all the meat has been rolled (makes about 25). Then place the meatballs in a single layer in the skillet. Make sure they are covered with boiling water.

Boil for 3 minutes or until the meat turns dark. Remove from the skillet and drain well.

To finish the cooking, simmer the meatballs in the tomato sauce for 15 or so minutes.

❋

The kids are very proud of how sophisticated their tastes are. One day Rose came back from school on a Friday, when the students bring their own lunches, and told me, "You know, Marta, I am the only one in my class who knows about orrechiette with broccoli and garlic."

❋

Summer Spaghetti Salad

Serves 4 to 6

16 ounces mozzarella cheese
5 ripe tomatoes, peeled, seeded, and coarsely chopped
1 cup fresh basil leaves, coarsely chopped
1 large clove garlic, pressed
2 Tablespoons salt
1 Tablespoon olive oil
16 ounces thin spaghetti
Salt and pepper

Bring a large pot of water to a boil.

Cut the mozzarella into small cubes and set aside in a small bowl. Combine the tomatoes, basil, and garlic in another bowl.

When the water is boiling hard, add 2 tablespoons salt and the oil. Add the spaghetti and cook just until it is al dente. Do not overcook.

Quickly drain the spaghetti and return it at once to the warm pot. Immediately stir in the mozzarella; the heat of the pasta will melt it slightly. Stir in the contents of the other bowl. Season to taste with salt and pepper.

Transfer to a serving bowl and serve at room temperature.

Lemon Pound Cake

16 Tablespoons (2 sticks) butter, softened
1⅓ cups sugar
2 eggs
1½ cups flour
½ teaspoon salt
½ cup evaporated milk
Zest and juice of 1 lemon (This is easier to do if you grate first, then squeeze.)

Preheat the oven to 350°. Butter an 8 x 4-inch loaf pan.

Beat together the butter and sugar until light and fluffy, then beat in the eggs, one at a time. Combine the flour and salt and add a third to the butter-sugar mixture. Add half the evaporated milk, then half of the remaining dry ingredients, the rest of the milk, and the rest of the dry ingredients. Stir in the lemon zest and juice, then pour the batter into the prepared pan.

Bake for 45 minutes. The cake will be shrinking in from the sides of the pan.

Let the cake cool for a few minutes in the pan, then turn out onto a rack. Turn the cake over to finish cooling right side up. Serve 1 or 2 slices per portion.

Madam, Caroline, Ed, and Anthony looking through a scrapbook.

10
OCTOBER

Back to New York: Fall Meals

By October the children were in school, and we were settled back into our city life. Later, when the children were older, Madam would go to Virginia to hunt. She had a little house down there and would ride all the time and live a very plain life.

I usually didn't go because she didn't really need me. The house was small and the housekeeper could cook simple meals for Madam if she wanted them. But she liked being by herself, and one year she came back, so proud, and told me she had discovered something great; it was called Lean Cuisine. She couldn't get over that you just had to put one in the oven and after a short time you took it out and there was everything from soup to dessert. She thought that was great.

That was the thing about Madam and food. She was very refined about it the way she was about everything, but it wasn't really what she was most interested in. She wanted to give the best to her family and guests, but for herself she would be satisfied with the same plain food every day as long as it was good.

It wasn't that the food we served guests was fancier. It's just that it was served differently. If Madam was alone or there was just family, a risotto with seafood or salmon and a salad would be a good light dinner. But for guests the risotto might be the first course of a more formal meal.

Because she wanted good things served at her table, she would always be on the lookout for new, interesting food when she was eating in restaurants. She would come home and say to me she had eaten something so good that day for lunch and could I make the same thing. I would say, "Maybe, Madam, but what was it?" And then she would start to tell me, and perhaps she would say, "Well, it was sort of in a light brownish sauce that was delicious." And I would ask what she thought might have been in that sauce, and she would think and say, "Maybe mushrooms." So I would ask what the sauce was served with, and Madam would say it was a little piece of something, sort of square, and it might have been some chicken or maybe veal, but it tasted wonderful. I would keep asking questions and get as much information as I could and then try to duplicate what she had eaten and liked. When I did—because I knew her tastes so well—she was always amazed and grateful. That is what made anything I did for her worthwhile. It was my pleasure to please her.

When we were back in New York, it was time to start the more formal kind of entertaining. Every morning Madam and I would start the day discussing what needed to be taken care of that day and, if people were coming for dinner, what I should cook. At the start, when I was first cooking, Madam would give me menus and cookbooks with the recipes she liked and explain exactly how she wanted everything. But after a while she knew that I understood perfectly and would mostly leave it to me. For instance, I knew Madam didn't like to have to deal with cutting her food. She wanted just to be able to pick up a fork and start eating. And I knew she didn't want to spend too long at the table, so food shouldn't be complicated to eat. And I knew how much she loved ice cream but that she didn't want to eat it too much and if there were guests and we were having dessert, she would like some fruit dessert that would also look pretty. Strawberries are wonderful on their own, but I would also serve them mixed with slices of kiwi and black grapes because the colors and textures are so pretty together.

A lot of years when we got back from the Vineyard, I would leave and go to Europe to visit my family in Italy and my French family in France. Before I went I would explain to whoever was going to be doing the cooking the same sorts of things Madam had once

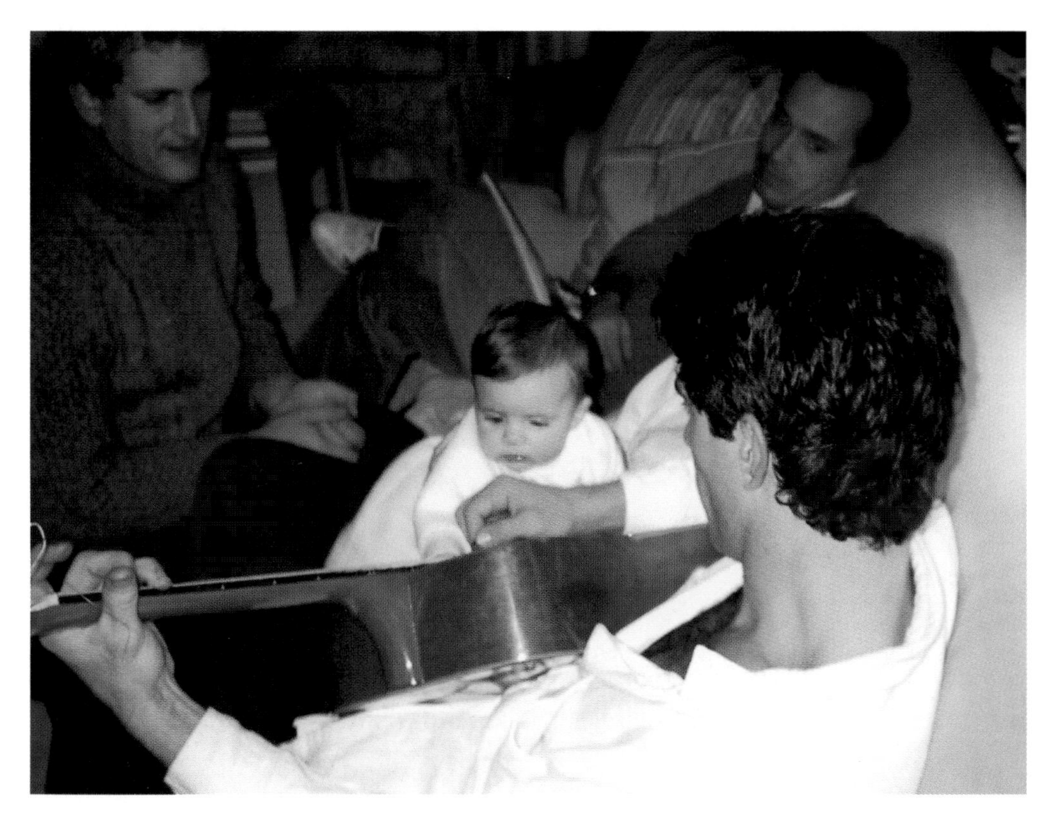

Five-month-old Rose accepting aqdoration, admiration, and a seranade from her father, cousin, and uncle.

explained to me, and gave them menus and cookbooks. But when I got back, Madam would always tell me that she didn't understand but somehow So and So's veal didn't taste as good as mine, even though she was working from the same recipe.

Maybe that's because if you cook all the time you get to know exactly the tastes of the people you are cooking for and also you know the recipes and have confidence. For instance, when I am making a sauce, I will often have four cups of stock on hand but only use two or three. But I want to make sure I have more in case I need it, so I write down the bigger amount. Also, because by now I know food and especially the food I make, I never taste as I cook. Sometimes I check at the end for salt, but I never taste as I go. I look at the food, and when it looks right to me I know it will be right. That comes from experience.

I am also very critical of myself and I have to think what I made is perfect. I have found that other people don't have the same standards. In the beginning, sometimes I would make something that I thought wasn't right, but I had to serve it anyway because of time or because there was nothing else or for whatever reason. That was the dish I would always get a lot of compliments on. Of course, it was still good ingredients. It just wasn't to my standards.

Sorrel and Potato Soup

Serves 6 to 8

4 Tablespoons (½ stick) butter
1 large onion, peeled and sliced thin
2 medium potatoes, peeled and sliced thin
8 cups fresh sorrel leaves
4 cups chicken stock (see page 132)
Salt and pepper
1 cup light cream

Melt the butter in a large pot. Add the onion and cook over medium heat, stirring often, for 5 minutes or until it is softened. Add the potatoes and continue to cook and stir for another 10 minutes. Add the sorrel and keep stirring it until it has wilted. Then add the stock, cover, and cook until the onions and potatoes are soft.

Remove the soup from the heat, season with salt and pepper, and let cool. Puree in batches in a food processor. Don't use a blender; you want some pieces left. Return the puree to the pot and stir in the cream.

When you are ready to serve, reheat the soup to the boiling point, correct the seasonings, and serve immediately.

Coulibiac with Bass in Phyllo

Serves 2

STUFFING

¼ cup dry white wine

2 teaspoons quick-cooking tapioca

1 hard-boiled egg

2 yolks of hard-boiled eggs

⅔ cup cooked rice

3 Tablespoons dill, snipped with scissors. (Save a sprig to garnish the finished dish.)

Salt and white pepper

FISH

12 ounces striped bass fillets, skinned

Salt and white pepper

2 Tablespoons olive oil

PASTRY

4 sheets phyllo pastry. (You can buy this now, prepared, in most supermarkets.)

8 Tablespoons (1 stick) butter, melted and cooled

Heat the wine in a small saucepan. Remove the pan from the heat, add the tapioca, and let soak for 5 minutes.

(continued on next page)

Chop the hard-boiled egg and the yolks and put them into a bowl with the rice and snipped dill. Stir in the tapioca and season with salt and white pepper.

Cut the striped bass into 4 pieces, each more or less 3½ by 2 inches. Season with salt and white pepper. Heat 2 tablespoons oil in a skillet over moderately high heat and sear each piece of fish for 30 seconds on each side. As you remove each piece from the pan, put it onto a plate and let it cool.

Wet 2 dish towels, then wring them out so they are barely damp. Lay one out on the work surface, lay the 4 sheets of phyllo on the towel, cover with the second towel.

Preheat the oven to 375°. Butter a baking sheet.

Remove the towel from over the phyllo and lift the top sheet off the stack. Spread it flat on the counter. Brush with some of the cooled melted butter, cover with a second phyllo sheet, and brush that sheet with more butter. Fold the pastry in half, short end to short end, and brush with more butter.

Place a quarter of the filling in the center of the phyllo and top it with a piece of fish. Top the fish with another layer of filling and a second piece of fish. Bring the 2 short ends of the phyllo together and fold them under around the fish and filling. Fold under the two remaining open ends to form a neat package, then place the package carefully on the buttered baking sheet.

Assemble a second package the same way, using the remaining pastry, filling, and fish, and place it next to the first on the baking sheet. Brush the coulibiacs with the rest of the melted butter and bake for 20 to 25 minutes until they are puffed and golden.

Transfer the coulibiacs to a heated serving dish, garnish with the reserved sprig of dill, and serve with Beurre Blanc (recipe follows).

Beurre Blanc

Makes 1½ cups

¼ cup white wine vinegar
¼ cup dry white wine
1 Tablespoon very finely minced shallots
24 Tablespoons (3 sticks) butter, chilled and cut into small pieces
Salt and pepper
Lemon juice to taste

In a medium-sized nonreactive saucepan (enamel or stainless steel), combine the wine, vinegar, and shallots and boil down to about 1½ tablespoons.

Remove pan from the heat and immediately begin beating in 1 or 2 little pieces of the butter, using a wire whisk. As the butter begins melting into the liquid, beat in another piece or two.

Return the pan to the burner over very low heat and continue to whisk in little pieces of butter. Keep whisking constantly and add the next piece of butter as the previous one begins to incorporate into the sauce. When you have finished, the sauce will be thick, the consistency of a light Hollandaise.

When the last piece of butter has been incorporated, immediately remove the pan from the heat and beat in seasonings to taste. The Beurre Blanc should be served immediately in a slightly warm bowl.

Medallions of Veal with Chive Sauce

Serves 6 to 8

1 small loin of veal (about 3 pounds), boned and trimmed
8 Tablespoons (1 stick) butter, clarified (see pages 152–53)
4 medium carrots, peeled
4 medium white turnips, peeled
2 large cucumbers, peeled and seeded
½ cup port wine
½ cup chopped chives
Salt and pepper

Slice the veal into eight 1½-inch-thick pieces.

Circle the circumference of each medallion with a piece of kitchen string and tighten it to hold the meat firm. Refrigerate.

Pare the vegetables into 2-inch-long olive shapes.

Bring a small saucepan of salted water to a boil. Separately blanch the carrots and the turnips just until almost tender. Drain and keep cool. The cucumbers should stay raw. Refrigerate all the vegetables.

All of this can be done in advance, so that the final preparation of this dish is very quick. When you are ready to continue, bring the veal and vegetables to room temperature.

Preheat the oven to 300°.

Lightly coat a medium skillet with about ¼ cup of the clarified butter. Brown both sides of the veal medallions quickly over high heat. Then remove them to another pan and keep them warm in the oven.

Heat the rest of the clarified butter in another saucepan, and quickly sauté the vegetables all together.

Meanwhile, deglaze the veal pan with the port wine, scraping up all the bits of meat. Sprinkle in the chives and swirl the sauce around. Season to taste.

Quickly arrange the medallions, overlapping, down the middle of a platter and arrange the sautéed vegetables on either side. Pour the chive sauce over the meat and serve at once.

Madam didn't like any food to be too rich or fattening, so I would substitute with lighter ingredients when possible. For instance, I made what I guess is a version of a POTATOES GRATIN, but in between the layers of thinly sliced potatoes I used a little good olive oil and, of course, salt and pepper. The oil was instead of all that butter and still tasted very good.

I did another version, VEGETABLES GRATIN. I'd put a tiny bit of oil in the bottom of a baking dish, then over it a layer of very thinly sliced zucchini with dill. Then another little sprinkle of oil, then maybe a thin layer of tomatoes with basil. A little more oil, then perhaps some thin slices of eggplant with thyme. More oil and then some thinly sliced Vidalia onions. I kept adding layers of vegetables and their herbs and a little oil until I got to the top of the dish. It came out so tasty when it was baked.

Pêches Cardinal

Serves 4

8 ripe peaches
1½ cups sugar
Juice of ½ lemon
1 cinnamon stick
2 Tablespoons coarsely chopped pistachio nuts

Choose a pot wide enough that all the peaches can be in one layer and deep enough that they can be covered by liquid. Using the pot as a pattern, cut out a circle of waxed paper the size of the inner circumference.

Arrange the unpeeled peaches in the pot. Add the sugar, lemon juice, and cinnamon stick. Pour in cold water to cover, then place the waxed paper disk over the top and bring to a boil. Lower the heat, cover the pot, and simmer 15 to 20 minutes until the peaches are soft enough to be pierced easily with the point of a sharp knife.

Let the peaches cool in the liquid.

When they are cool, slip the skins off with the help of a small knife.

To serve, pour some Raspberry Sauce (recipe follows) into the bottom of a serving bowl or a platter with a high rim. Arrange the peaches on the sauce and dribble more over the tops, then sprinkle with the pistachios.

Serve at room temperature with the rest of the Raspberry Sauce in a bowl passed at the table.

Raspberry Sauce

Makes 1½ to 2 cups

1 pint fresh raspberries
Juice of ½ lemon
½ cup sugar
½ teaspoon arrowroot
1 Tablespoon Framboise (a raspberry-flavored liqueur) or Kirsch (a cherry-flavored liqueur)

Combine the raspberries, lemon juice, and ¼ cup water in a food processor or blender and puree until smooth. Strain through a fine sieve to remove all the seeds.

Pour the puree into a small pan, add the sugar, and bring to a boil. Then reduce the heat and simmer for 15 minutes, stirring occasionally. Dissolve the arrowroot in the liqueur and stir into the sauce. Remove from the heat and let cool. When cool, cover and refrigerate.

This can be made with frozen raspberries, but in the summer, when fresh berries are available, it tastes so much better.

This sauce is also wonderful with Frozen Lemon Soufflé.

Tarte Tatin

Serves 4 to 6

I make this in a French cake pan that is 10 inches in diameter and about 2 inches deep. They are available in good cooking equipment stores. But any pan with high sides and more or less the same capacity will do if it can be put on a burner and also into the oven.

PÂTE SUCRÉE

½ cup sugar
2½ cups flour
1 egg, lightly beaten
8 Tablespoons (1 stick) butter, melted

Mix together the sugar and flour. Stir in the egg and beat until combined, then stir in the melted butter and mix well until the dough forms a ball. Wrap in waxed paper and refrigerate for half an hour.

Preheat the oven to 350°.

FILLING

14 Tablespoons (1¾ sticks) butter
1 cup sugar
1 teaspoon vanilla extract
8 Golden Delicious apples, peeled, cored, and cut into quarters

Melt the butter in the pan over high heat. Add half the sugar and the vanilla, turn the heat down to low, and let cook for a minute until it bubbles. When that happens arrange the chunks of apple in a circle around the edge of the pan, then fill in the middle with the other chunks.

Pour the rest of the sugar over the apples, raise the heat to medium, and cook until a caramel forms under the apples. Turn off heat.

Remove the pastry from the refrigerator. Flour a piece of waxed paper, place the pastry on it. Roll into a round a little larger than the pan. Use the paper to pick up the circle of pastry and flop it onto the apples. Cut off any excess beyond the rim, make a few slits to let steam escape, and put into the preheated oven.

Bake for 1 hour or until the crust is golden.

While the tart is baking, rinse a dish towel in cold water and refrigerate it.

When the tart is ready, remove it from the oven and place it on the cold, damp dish towel. Let stand for 2 minutes, then put the pan on a burner and cook over high heat for just 30 seconds.

Take the pan off the stove and cover with a round serving plate. Carefully (because some of the caramel will have liquefied) turn them over together and remove the mold.

Keep the tart warm and serve with Crème Fraîche.

Warm Apple Tart

Serves 4

This is a much lighter tart than the Tarte Tatin. It is a good dessert to serve after a big dinner or for a lunch.

In order to make this you will need an 8-inch cake pan with a removable bottom.

PASTRY

6 Tablespoons (¾ stick) cold butter, cut into small pieces
1 cup sifted flour
1 Tablespoon ice water
Pinch of salt

APPLES

2 to 3 McIntosh apples

Put the pieces of butter into the bowl of an electric mixer. Sift in the flour, then add the water and salt and beat briefly until the mixture is mealy. At least once turn the mixer off and use a rubber spatula to scrape the ingredients back down the sides of the bowl.

Turn the mixture out onto a piece of waxed paper. Gather the corners of the paper together, then press the dough together with your hands (through the paper) until it forms a ball.

Put the ball of dough onto a floured board and knead until the ingredients are all combined and no bits of butter show. Don't overknead though and don't let it get sticky. Gather the dough into a ball, drop it into a plastic bag, and refrigerate for at least half an hour.

Preheat the oven to 425°.

When the pastry is chilled, reflour the board and the pastry and roll the pastry out into a round about 8½ inches in diameter. Then, using the bottom of the pan as a pattern, cut the pastry into a neat circle the right size. Fit the pastry into the bottom of the pan.

Peel and core the apples and slice them into thin half circles. Starting in the middle of the pastry, arrange the slices in a pinwheel pattern. The apples should cover the pastry completely so that no edge shows.

Bake for 45 minutes. While the tart is baking, prepare the Apricot Sauce (recipe follows) and warm a round serving platter.

Another way to make this is, instead of serving with the Apricot Sauce, melt about 2 tablespoons of a good apricot preserve—Bon Maman or Polaner or Hero—in a small saucepan with a little bit of water. Stir until it becomes a thick syrup and then use it to glaze the tart.

Apricot Sauce

1 (16-ounce) can unsweetened apricot halves, drained
½ cup water
1 vanilla bean
2 Tablespoons sugar

Simmer all the ingredients together in a saucepan for 15 minutes or until the sauce is reduced by about one-third. It should be the consistency of a medium-thick marmalade.

Remove the vanilla bean and puree the sauce in a blender. Keep warm.

When the tart is baked, take it out of the oven and with a rubber spatula spread a film of apricot sauce over the apples. Remove the tart from the pan by pushing the bottom up, then slide the tart off the bottom onto the warm platter. Cut into quarters and serve immediately. Pass the warm sauce with it.

This is John's ninth birthday, I think, with one of those fabulous cakes I didn't make.

11
November

Thanksgiving and the Children's Birthdays

John's birthday is November 25 and Caroline's the twenty-seventh. We always celebrated them separately and always over the Thanksgiving weekend, even if that meant we had to cheat a little and have one party a day early or late.

We had a house in New Jersey where we went most weekends with the kids unless we were going somewhere with Mr. and Mrs. Onassis. For a while we had a rented house, but Mr. Onassis didn't like it, so in 1974 they bought a much nicer one. He didn't come often because he was more a city person, but I remember he did come for the Thanksgiving/birthday weekend that first year. He arrived after everyone else had eaten and was having dinner in the kitchen. At one point he asked me to pass him the salt, and I picked it up and tried to hand it to him, but he told me no, put it down on the table. So I did and then he picked it up and used it. He said, "If you hand someone salt, you will have a fight with them, and I don't want to be fighting with you." Ever since then, I don't ever give anyone salt directly; I put it down for them to pick up.

When the children were young, we all drove to New Jersey together on the Wednesday before Thanksgiving. But later, when they could drive themselves, Madam and I drove down on Wednesday and brought a lot of the food with us because you

Ed and Anthony watch Caroline blowing out the candles on her twenty-fifth birthday. There was a big party, so this was one of the few birthdays we celebrated in New York.

couldn't get it as good out there. We always brought fish if we were going to have it, and usually meat. And we always brought good fruit and breads. In the early days I wasn't cooking, but we still brought the food.

Also, during the time John was growing so much, I would have to bring two of everything for him in bigger sizes. All the riding stuff stayed out there, but I would buy the new things before we left New York.

Everyone got there before dinner on Wednesday. As soon as Madam and I arrived, she would go riding. Then when she was back and everybody was there we all had dinner together and went to bed early.

The next morning, Thanksgiving, was the opening day of the hunt. We had breakfast more or less together in the kitchen. Everyone was always rushing in and out, looking for something. I remember Madam saying, "Now, Jacqueline, where did you leave those gloves?" She only called herself Jacqueline when she was scolding herself. I would be up and down, looking for the lost items. Madam always said if I couldn't find something, it really was lost. I have always been able to find things. I find four-leaf clovers all the time, lots of them.

We ate more or less the same breakfast we did Christmas morning, but that was peaceful and this wasn't. They had to be at the stable for the opening of the hunt.

They never got the fox. There was no fox. Mrs. Onassis explained this to me because I was upset and asked her how she could kill a little thing like that. She told me they just put the scent of a fox around and then the dogs go and find it. It's called a drag because they drag a bag with the fox scent, and the hunt is just for fun. In France it's different. When they hunt, they kill a deer or a boar, and then they chop it up. It's a big ceremony.

Once I went to a *corrida* in Spain. I had never been to one and I was very upset when they killed four bulls. They kill them with that sword at the end. And that poor animal just

Madam, Caroline, and John before the hunt. Ed doesn't hunt, but he's a very loyal follower.

Madam on a Thanksgiving weekend in New Jersey with Tatiana and Greenie, the barn cat.

lay down there and died, and the people all clapped. I only went once. I didn't ever want to go again.

Madam and the children would come back around one or one-thirty, and even though they were hungry from riding, they would have a light lunch: minestrone soup, maybe pasta or a frittata, bread, salad, fruit. Because that evening we would have the regular Thanksgiving dinner. I loved doing it because if you prepare the food yourself, you are not only participating in your special way, you are also giving the people you cook for a special gift of yourself.

We always had sweet potatoes with marshmallows, creamed onions, peas, string beans, and two kinds of cranberry sauce: the kind with berries cooked up with sugar, and also the jelly. There was also a green salad with mushrooms and tomatoes if I could find good ones. And, of course, the turkey. I always started by boiling up the neck and giblets and other parts we weren't going to eat to make a stock to moisten the stuffing. The stuffing had dried bread cubes, celery, mushrooms, chestnuts, onions, sausage, and parsley. Then after we had a pumpkin and a mince pie I brought from the city. Those were served with vanilla ice cream.

When I first was cooking Thanksgiving dinner, I had never made CREAMED ONIONS, but I had eaten them before. So I thought about how they looked and tasted and said to myself they were in a béchamel. So I peeled two baskets of those little pearl onions and put them in a baking dish with a stick of butter. Then I covered the dish and cooked the onions on top of the stove until they were golden and soft. They shouldn't get brown. Those little onions don't fall apart; they just get soft.

Then I made a béchamel sauce with flour, butter, hot milk, salt, and white pepper and cooked it a little so there wouldn't be a taste of the flour. When the onions were ready, I poured the sauce over them and left them in the sauce until I reheated them together.

I already said we would celebrate John's birthday and Caroline's on two different days. For that meal the birthday girl or boy got to choose what we would eat and then I would make a birthday cake for each party: always one chocolate and one something else, like a white or yellow cake. And for Caroline I would make the Gingerbread Ring too. But there had to be a birthday cake. Then we would have the kid's special favorite other dessert—Chocolate Roll for Caroline and Floating Island for John with lunch on the birthday.

The children usually left on Sunday. When they were young, they had school Monday, and when they were older, they had other things to do. Madam always left on Monday. Usu-

John loves hats, so it's a family tradition to give him a new one every birthday.

ally everyone rode again on Friday and Saturday, and then I think there was another hunt on Sunday.

Even when Mrs. Onassis wasn't there, we went to New Jersey, the kids and I, and they rode every weekend. Caroline much more. John was very allergic to horses at that time. He couldn't stay near them without sneezing. He grew out of it and is fine now.

They had a couple of horses who stayed with the neighbors, and Caroline especially rode all fall and winter when she could. She rides very well. But one time I remember she was riding and a branch hit her forehead and she had a big crack. We had to go to the hospital in New Jersey so they could put in some stitches. But she was fine. She had no concussion. She still rides now. So do her daughters, every weekend on Long Island. Jack is too young. The girls go twice on the weekends, both Saturday and Sunday. They are terrific and they love it.

In the evenings on those long weekends, we would watch old movies I would also bring from New York, like *Mildred Pierce* or *Some Like It Hot.* We watched one a night. We had a projector and a screen out there that only John knew how to run. It was very relaxed and very family. Mostly it was just us, which usually included Anthony Radziwill. It makes me both happy and sad to think about those Thanksgivings—happy because we had so much fun, and sad because they are over. But things have to move along.

MINESTRONE

Serves 8

There are many different minestrones; this is just one version.

¼ cup olive oil
2 Tablespoons (¼ stick) butter
¾ cup sliced yellow onions

1 cup diced carrots

1 cup diced celery

1 cup peeled and diced potatoes

1½ cups fresh white beans

1½ cups diced zucchini

1 cup flat green beans, cut into ½-inch pieces

3 cups thinly sliced spinach leaves

3 ripe medium tomatoes, chopped

6 cups homemade meat stock (see page 78) (or use 2 cups canned beef broth and 4 cups water)

¼ cup each chopped basil, dill, and parsley

Salt

½ cup fresh Parmesan cheese, grated just before it is used

Choose a pot large enough to hold all these ingredients. Heat the oil and butter in it, then add the sliced onions, and cook over low heat until the onions wilt.

Add the diced carrots and cook for 2 minutes, then add, in order, each of the other vegetables through the green beans. Let each cook, stirring, for a few minutes before adding the next. Finally, stir in the shredded spinach and the chopped tomatoes and cook for about 5 more minutes, stirring often.

Add the stock, the herbs, and salt to taste. Cover and cook at a very slow boil for at least 2 hours. Minestrone should never be watery, so cook until it is soupy thick. If it seems to be becoming too thick, add more stock or water.

Just before serving, swirl in grated Parmesan cheese. Or serve it separately so people can add as much or as little as they want.

Green Risotto

Serves 4 as a main course

I loved to serve this for lunch in winter because it was food with such a beautiful color.

½ cup olive oil
1 medium onion, finely chopped
1½ cups arborio rice
5 cups chicken stock (see page 132)
½ cup white wine
10 leaves fresh spinach

Heat the olive oil in a heavy 3-quart saucepan. Add the onion and sauté until golden brown, then add the rice and cook for a minute or so, stirring so that each grain is coated with oil. Meanwhile, heat the stock. Add the wine to the rice and cook until it has evaporated, then start adding the stock. Pour in a little at a time, just enough so the rice is covered, then cook, stirring constantly, until the stock has been absorbed. Continue to add stock until the rice is the right consistency—al dente. This should take about 20 minutes. Begin tasting after about 15 minutes. You may not use all the stock, but judge by the texture of the rice, not the amount of liquid.

Wash the spinach leaves, then put them, still wet, into a blender and liquefy them. You may need to add a tiny bit more water. Add the puree to the rice and stir it in. The rice will become a nice green color.

Serve at once with Parmesan cheese.

FRITTATA

You can use all different fillings in any amount you want to make a frittata. If you want to make one with vegetables, you can use zucchini, beans, spinach, whatever. But there is always a tomato sauce. My formula is that for 6 people, I use 10 eggs and then as many vegetables as seem right.

I like to make my frittatas in a high pan because if the serving is higher, you feel you are eating enough. The pan should also be able to go on a burner and under the broiler. An old-fashioned iron skillet is good.

Peel and seed enough tomatoes to make a sauce, then stew them in a little olive oil in an uncovered pan for 1 hour or until they are reduced. At the end of their cooking, add chopped basil and salt and pepper.

The vegetables, whichever ones you choose, should be precooked in a pan with olive oil. When the vegetables are cooked, mix them with the tomato sauce.

In another bowl, beat the eggs together.

Heat some olive oil in the ovenproof pan, then pour in first the eggs, then the tomato mixture. Cook on top of the stove *very* slowly. Keep checking. The eggs should start to thicken, but the top has to stay liquid. As soon as it has achieved that state, run the pan under the broiler to harden and crisp the top.

To serve, which you should do immediately, invert the frittata onto a heated platter and decorate it with herb sprigs. I like this on a white platter because I think that china with a design takes away from your design on the food.

Chocolate Roll

Serves 6 to 8

There is no flour in this recipe, so rolling the cake can be tricky. I usually make two so I'm sure I'll have one that looks good.

ROLL

6 ounces semisweet chocolate

3 Tablespoons milk

5 eggs, separated

¾ cup sugar

¼ teaspoon salt

FILLING

2 cups heavy cream, whipped and sweetened with ½ cup confectioners' sugar

or

1 quart vanilla ice cream

Preheat the oven to 350°.

Butter a 15½ x 10½-inch jelly roll pan. Line with a piece of waxed paper, then butter the paper.

Melt the chocolate with the milk in the top of a double boiler. Let cool a little.

While it is cooling, beat together the egg yolks and sugar until they are pale and thick. When they are the right consistency and the chocolate is warm, mix the chocolate into the yolks.

In a separate, clean bowl, beat the whites until they are foamy, then add the salt and

(continued on next page)

continue beating until the whites hold soft peaks. Gently fold one-third of the whites into the chocolate mixture. When they are incorporated, lightly fold in the rest of the whites.

Spread the batter evenly over the waxed paper in the jelly roll pan and bake for about 20 minutes or until a toothpick poked into the middle comes out clean.

Remove the cake from the oven and turn it out onto a clean cloth kitchen towel spread on a counter. Remove the paper and trim any crisp edges off the cake. Starting from one of the long sides, use the towel to roll the cake up around the towel. Let it rest, rolled, for a minute, then unroll. Let it rest, unrolled, for another minute, then reroll in the towel and let it rest to cool completely.

Unroll again and spread with the sweetened whipped cream. Reroll without the towel and dust the top with confectioner's sugar. Refrigerate until ready to serve.

This can also be spread with softened vanilla ice cream, then rerolled and stored in the freezer until ready to serve. If you use ice cream, serve the roll with Hot Chocolate Sauce.

Hot Chocolate Sauce

Makes about 1 cup

2 ounces dark, bittersweet eating chocolate, grated
4 Tablespoons (1/2 stick) butter
1/4 cup unsweetened cocoa
3/4 cup sugar
1/2 cup heavy cream or sour cream
1 teaspoon flavoring: vanilla or brandy or liquid coffee

Melt the grated chocolate with the butter over low heat, stirring occasionally.

Add the cocoa and sugar and stir vigorously until blended.

Stir in the cream, either heavy or sour, then stir in the flavoring.

This sauce can be made in advance and reheated over low heat until it bubbles slightly before serving. Any leftovers can be stored in the refrigerator.

Gingerbread Ring

Serves 6 to 8

I make this in a big 11-cup Bundt pan that is 11 inches for the outside diameter and the hole in the middle is about 3½ inches wide. The batter, when it is poured in, will only come about halfway up, but as it cooks, it will rise to almost fill the pan. I like this pan because it has a pretty big hole, and that is where you will be putting applesauce. But you can use any tube or Bundt pan that holds the same amount.

8 Tablespoons (1 stick) butter
1 cup sugar
2 eggs
¾ cup boiling water
¾ cup molasses
2½ cups flour
2 teaspoons baking soda
½ teaspoon salt
4 teaspoons ground ginger
Applesauce
2 cups heavy cream, whipped and sweetened with ½ cup confectioners' sugar

Preheat the oven to 350°.

Butter and lightly flour an 11-cup Bundt or tube pan and set it aside.

In a large bowl, cream the butter. Add the sugar and beat until fluffy. Add the eggs and beat them in well, then add the boiling water and molasses and stir until completely blended in.

Sift the flour, baking soda, salt, and ginger together and beat into the butter mixture. Pour the batter into the prepared pan and bake for 40 to 45 minutes or just until a toothpick inserted into the center comes out clean. Don't overbake.

Let the cake cool in the pan for about 5 minutes, then turn it out onto a large plate and fill the center hole with applesauce. When you serve this, pass with a bowl of sweetened whipped cream and another of applesauce.

As Caroline makes her wish after blowing out the candles on her gingerbread ring, I'm waiting to give her her birthday cake.

Floating Island

Serves 8

This dessert has always been John's favorite. It has to be served for his birthday and as many other times of year as he can talk me into it.

1 vanilla bean
2 cups milk
8 eggs, separated (make sure they are very fresh)
1⅓ cups sugar

CARAMEL
½ cup sugar

Scrape seeds from the vanilla bean into the milk in a small saucepan. Bring to a boil, then turn off the heat, cover the pan, and set aside.

In a medium saucepan, combine the 8 yolks with half the sugar. Beat until the mixture lightens in color and a ribbon forms.

Place the saucepan over low heat and add the flavored milk. Stir constantly with a wooden spoon. As soon as the cream thickens and coats the spoon, remove the pan from the heat. Do not let the custard come to a boil.

Immediately force the custard through a fine sieve into a bowl and stir until it cools. When it is completely cool, cover and refrigerate until you are ready to serve.

Place 8 egg whites in a stainless steel bowl and beat until they are firm. At that point, begin adding the remaining half of the 1⅓ cups sugar a little at a time, beating constantly so the whites remain very light.

Fill a large, low pan: a sautoir or skillet three-quarters full of water. Bring the water to the boil, then lower the heat so that it stays at a simmer. Use 2 wooden spoons to form large ovals each about ½ cup of the beaten whites. Very gently place each oval as it is made into the simmering water and poach for about 1 to 2 minutes. Turn the ovals in the water so that all sides cook.

Remove from water when just firm and drain either on a cloth or in a flat fine-meshed sieve placed over a bowl. Let cool.

While the islands are cooling, melt the ½ cup of sugar for the caramel in a stainless steel or aluminum pot with a pouring lip. Stir constantly so it doesn't burn. When it has melted and become a light brown and smells like caramel, it is ready. Sugar is easy to burn, so watch and stir carefully. If you melted the sugar ahead of time and it hardens, you can remelt it carefully over water.

Then I pull a spoonful of the caramel out of the pot and let it fall over a stick—the handle of a wooden spoon or anything like that—so that it makes strings. Put the strings, as they are made, carefully on a plate. Stop when you have a big tumbleweed of them.

Pour the cold custard into a large deep-sided dish. Float the egg whites on the top, then drop snarls of caramel over them so it looks like a big dandelion head. Serve. Sometimes the caramel starts to melt a little and the brown makes you just want to dig a spoon in right away.

Christmas Eve dinner.

12

DECEMBER

Christmas Day Breakfast

We'd eat late, about ten or ten-thirty, before noon mass. After the kids were grown and lived on their own, we ate when everybody got there. We had had the big dinner the night before at about eight and maybe gone to mass if we weren't too tired.

Christmas dinner was very festive. We would have the family, of course, and then cousins or friends, sometimes as many as ten people. Dinner wasn't turkey because we had just had it a few weeks before for Thanksgiving, so we'd have veal or lamb, which Madam liked. And always the traditional desserts: bûche de noël and croquembouche. I have made them, but usually I was too busy with everything else, so I had Les Delices du Côte Basque, where they did very good work, make them for me.

The first year I ordered them, I remember I explained very clearly that I didn't want a lot of decoration. Madam liked things plain, plain, plain. They should look nice but not be all fancy. The croquembouche was delivered, but I didn't have a chance to open it until I had finished with the main course. Then I opened the box and I was horrified.

I don't know what they thought was no decoration, but it wasn't what I thought. I quickly had to tear off angels and bells and ribbons and stars. They were all over. But

Christmas Eve dinner with the family.

then everywhere I had pulled off a decoration, there was a little hole in the caramel. I had to rush and get some hot water and a knife and carefully move the caramel around to cover the holes. But then where the caramel had been wet it got a little dull, not so shiny the way it should be. So I also had to quickly heat some sugar and make a little more caramel to patch.

That year, after I had cleaned up, I'm sure I was too tired to go to mass until the morning.

Especially in the last years, we didn't go until then. Madam and I still had to put out all the presents for everyone under the tree. She called it our "playing Santa." Everybody got a separate pile, and there were so many of us, and all the packages had to be arranged a certain way so it looked pretty. It couldn't look messy, and that took two hours at least.

So in the morning when everyone came, we'd have the stockings that had been hung the night before. This was done over breakfast. I had gotten up first to start the porridge. If

I knew when people were arriving, I'd have it ready. It was that Irish kind, McCann's, that comes in the tin and has texture and is kind of grainy. And it has to cook for an hour. When everyone was at the table, we'd have oatmeal with honey or maybe brown or white sugar and cream—everyone might want something a little different. The table would be set with a nice plain white cloth and maybe red or green ribbons to make it look festive. We sometimes used them if it was a small dinner Christmas Eve too. And the honey and sugar and cream would already be on the table along with fruit, always clementines and sometimes other fruit. We often had strawberries when we could get them, and sometimes maybe cut-up fruit. And there would be fresh-squeezed orange juice and grapefruit, prepared earlier in the morning so it was cold, for anyone who wanted it.

I cut up the grapefruit with my special knife. It could have been done with any knife, but I only liked to do it with that one. I cut the grapefruit in half, then cut around the sections the way you do, but then I cut around the middle and the outside and pulled. All the membrane came out in one piece and left just the sections in place.

Christmas breakfast with a centerpiece of lady apples.

Christmas morning. This is a very usual expression for Madam: biting her bottom lip.

Nothing else was done ahead of time and left waiting. When everyone finished the porridge, I served my Special Scrambled Eggs. I was making them while the family was eating the oatmeal. They are really regular fluffy scrambled eggs, but the family thought mine were the best. When John got married, I went with him and his bride, Carolyn, to spend Christmas with her family, and in the morning John asked if I would make my special scrambled eggs. I was so pleased that he still wanted them, and everyone seemed to love them.

With the eggs were all different kinds of nice toast. They were all from good breads: multigrain, country bread, English muffins. Everyone could have what they wanted when they wanted it. Often they all wanted different things. I kept it coming from the kitchen so it was always hot. I buttered it in the kitchen, one of those tricks I learned that made it more enjoyable for them. Otherwise, by the time they buttered the bread, it was cold and the butter didn't melt. The jams were already on the table with the honey: raspberry, John's favorite; strawberry, Caroline's favorite; as well as blueberry jam and marmalade. I put them each in a little dish with a little spoon. Never the jars on the table.

I kept coffee coming from the kitchen with hot milk. It was in the silver coffeepot, so it

stayed hot. Everyone drank coffee when the children got older. Before that, the children drank orange juice and the grownups drank coffee.

Sometimes, because I had the little containers, I made oeufs en cocotte. Those are individual servings of eggs each baked in a crock.

When John was young, he used to like me to make what we called SUNSHINE EGGS. That was a piece of toast with an egg yolk on it, then covered with beaten egg whites piped around the yolk and baked until the egg was done. It looked like a big yellow sun.

Then we would go to noon services if we hadn't been the night before and come home and open our presents. We would have lunch late, about one-thirty or two, because breakfast had been late and big. We'd usually just have soup and bread. I liked to serve borscht for its beautiful color. Or we might have quiche or risotto or tortellini. And with that we'd have a green salad, and for dessert, sweets left over from the night before if anyone wanted them, or Christmas cookies I'd made, or fruit. The cookies looked so cute in the bowl: the reindeer, the Christmas trees.

Finally, everyone would leave and that's when we separated, because the next day all of us always went away on vacation.

Marta's Special Scrambled Eggs

Serves 4 or 5

These instructions are for making the eggs in a double boiler. The size depends on how many eggs you are making. The eggs should be about 3 to 4 inches deep in the bottom of the pot. If they aren't deep enough, they cook too quickly, and if they are much deeper than that, they cook too slowly. Of course, if you are making eggs for a crowd, you may have to do them in batches.

4 Tablespoons (½ stick) cold unsalted butter, divided
8 to 10 eggs
¼ teaspoon salt
Pinch of pepper

Bring water to a boil in the bottom of the double boiler and melt 2 tablespoons of the butter in the top. When the butter is melted, use a fork or a wire whisk to beat the eggs in a bowl with the salt and pepper until the yolks and whites are absolutely homogenized. This is essential for the creamy finished product. But don't overbeat; treat the eggs the way you would if you were making an omelet.

Pour the beaten eggs into the butter, then stir and stir and stir slowly but all the time. I use a wooden spoon for this. After about 5 or 6 minutes, when nothing seems to be going on, the eggs will suddenly begin to thicken. When that happens, keep stirring, a little faster—the eggs have to be really stretched—for another minute or two.

When the eggs are the texture you want—we like them custardy and creamy—remove them from the heat and stir in the remaining 2 tablespoons of the cold butter. This will stop the cooking. Season to taste and serve right away. If the eggs get cold, they get stiff and lose their creaminess.

Risotto Primavera

Serves 4 to 6

This is called *primavera,* which means "spring" in Italian, because of the little vegetables. But the family liked to have it when it was cold outside.

5 Tablespoons olive oil, divided
2 cloves garlic, minced
4 plum tomatoes, peeled, seeded, and chopped
20 green beans, tips off and cut into ½-inch pieces
10 asparagus tips
2 medium zucchini, diced
6 cups chicken stock (see page 132)
1 large onion, chopped
2 cups arborio rice
½ cup fresh peas or thawed frozen baby peas
2 Tablespoons (¼ stick) butter
Salt and pepper

Heat 4 tablespoons of the olive oil in a skillet over low heat. Add the garlic, tomatoes, green beans, asparagus tips, and zucchini and sauté for 8 to 10 minutes. Remove from the heat and set aside.

In a saucepan, bring the stock to a steady simmer.

In a heavy 4-quart pot, heat the remaining tablespoon of olive oil. Add the onion and sauté until it begins to soften. Be careful not to let it brown. When the onion is ready, add the rice and stir with a wooden spoon for 1 minute to make sure all the grains are well coated with oil. Then begin to add the simmering stock ½ a cup at a time.

When the first of the stock has been added, stir the pot frequently and wait until the rice has almost completely absorbed the liquid before adding the next ½ cup. Keep stirring so the rice doesn't stick.

After about 20 minutes, begin tasting the rice and stop adding stock when the rice is al dente. There may be stock left over. Stir in the sautéed vegetables and the peas. Cook for another minute, stir in the butter, and season to taste with salt and pepper.

Serve immediately with a bowl of freshly grated Parmesan cheese on the table.

Pears Poached in Wine

Serves 4

1 (750-ml) bottle red wine
Juice of 1 lemon
1 vanilla bean, split
1½ cups sugar
8 pears

I use any pear that is good at the time. Usually I use Comice, but Bosc look very nice because they stand up high. I have also used Bartlett and Anjou and even Seckel, not the tiny ones but the slightly bigger ones.

In a saucepan large enough to hold all the pears, combine the wine, lemon juice, the vanilla bean, the sugar, and enough water to cover. Cover the pan and cook until the sugar has dissolved.

While that is going on bring a pot of water to a simmer. Blanch the pears for a minute or so, then immediately drop into cold water. Peel the skins off with your fingers or a small knife, leaving the stems in place.

Set the pears upright in the wine syrup and simmer until they are just tender. Use a wooden spoon to remove them from the pot so they don't bruise. Place them on a serving platter with sides to hold the liquid and refrigerate until ready to serve.

Raise the heat under the syrup and boil it until it is reduced by half. Let it cool to room temperature, then spoon it over the pears. Keep basting the pears over and over with the syrup. It will coat the pears beautifully and makes them all shiny and glazed.

Remove the pears from the refrigerator about 5 minutes before you are going to serve them so the syrup has a chance to get a little runny again.

AFTERWORD

It was hard for me to write this book because it brought back so many memories, good and bad. I kept remembering that Madam always was telling me I should write a cookbook so she could publish it herself. When that didn't work out, I lost heart for a while.

But Caroline and John kept pushing me in a nice way to get it done. Once I began to write Caroline read the manuscript and went over the pictures very seriously and made suggestions. I am with her and her family most weekends and when I prepared a dish for them and they thought it was good enough to go into the book, they always told me.

So, although Caroline decided to let John write the Foreword on his own, her encouragement must be as obvious as his on every page.

Recipe Index

(Page numbers in *italic* refer to illustrations.)